CW00950257

BFI TV Classics

BFI TV Classics is a series of books celebrating key individual television programmes and series. Television scholars, critics and novelists provide critical readings underpinned with careful research, alongside a personal response to the programme and a case for its 'classic' status.

Bleak House

Christine Geraghty

A BFI book published by Palgrave Macmillan

Images from *Bleak House*, © BBC

Whilst considerable effort has been made to correctly identify the copyright holders, this has not been possible in all cases. We apologise for any omissions or mistakes in the credits and we will endeavour to remedy, in future editions, errors brought to our attention by the relevant rights holder.

None of the content of this publication is intended to imply that it is endorsed by the programme's broadcaster or production companies involved.

First published in 2012 by
PALGRAVE MACMILLAN

on behalf of the

BRITISH FILM INSTITUTE
21 Stephen Street, London W1T 1LN
www.bfi.org.uk

There's more to discover about film and television through the BFI. Our world-renowned archive, cinemas, festivals, films, publications and learning resources are here to inspire you.

PALGRAVE MACMILLAN in the UK is an imprint of Macmillan Publishers Limited, registered in England, company number 785998, of Houndmills, Basingstoke, Hampshire RG21 6XS. Palgrave Macmillan in the US is a division of St Martin's Press LLC, 175 Fifth Avenue, New York, NY 10010. Palgrave Macmillan is the global academic imprint of the above companies and has companies and representatives throughout the world. Palgrave® and Macmillan® are registered trademarks in the United States, the United Kingdom, Europe and other countries.

Set by Cambrian Typesetters, Camberley, Surrey
Printed in China

This book is printed on paper suitable for recycling and made from fully managed and sustained forest sources. Logging, pulping and manufacturing processes are expected to conform to the environmental regulations of the country of origin.

British Library Cataloguing-in-Publication Data
A catalogue record for this book is available from the British Library
A catalog record for this book is available from the Library of Congress
10 9 8 7 6 5 4 3 2 1
21 20 19 18 17 16 15 14 13 12

ISBN 978–1–84457–417–9

Contents

Acknowledgments

This book is dedicated to my friends and colleagues in the Department of Theatre, Film and Television Studies at the University of Glasgow, including those in the Centre for Cultural Policy Research. The atmosphere created by staff and students in this inter-disciplinary department, where teaching was taken as seriously as research, contributed much to the development of my work on television and made it fun as well. Particular thanks to Amy Holdsworth for comments on an early draft of part of this book and to her and Karen Lury for conversations about what good television might be. I am grateful also to staff and students in the Department of Film and Television Studies at the University of Warwick for their very helpful questions and comments at a research seminar I gave there and in particular to Charlotte Brunsdon and Hannah Andrews for further suggestions and help. Conferences of the Association of Adaptation Studies have provided interesting and informative debates and particular thanks go to delegates at Istanbul who first heard about the 'problem of Esther'. Above all, I am grateful to Professor Grahame Smith who kindly read and commented on the first draft of this book; his enthusiasm for literature and cinema is exhilarating and his lifetime of scholarship on Dickens inspirational. Finally, my love and thanks to Paul Marks who read the penultimate draft and greatly helped to clarify what it was I was trying to say.

This book could have been twice as long without exhausting what there was to say so, more than usual, I have to confirm that omissions and errors are mine.

Introduction

This book is about a television classic, in a double sense. *Bleak House* (2005) qualifies as a classic serial in that it is an adaptation of a classic novel and follows in the long tradition of radio/television serials based on British nineteenth-century fiction.[1] But the classic serial has always reflected the time of its making and *Bleak House* also fits into the tradition of opening the source up to say different things and to attract new audiences at home and abroad. Examining this particular classic will allow us to look not only at this particular serial but at how the longstanding relationship between the venerable institutions of Charles Dickens and the BBC was faring in the early part of the twenty-first century.

    I will argue in this book that this combination of Dickens and the BBC opens up a range of issues which are pertinent to the way in which television fiction is produced and enjoyed 200 years after the author's birth. This is in part because Dickens himself so brilliantly exemplifies the professional practices and the challenges associated with popularity now faced by television. Dickens was a professional writer of a whole range of material; a magazine owner and a tireless editor; a theatrical enthusiast who made a huge success of readings from his own work. He wrote continuously, sometimes, at the beginning of his career, working on more than one book at a time, and was a hands-on editor and promoter of the writing of others. As a novelist, he reconciled ambitious claims for the value of literature with a commitment to popular serial publication and, in the process, transformed the practice

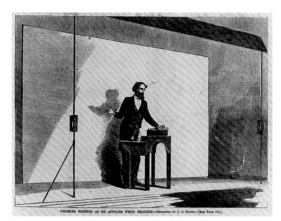

1. Charles Dickens as he appears when reading. Sketched by C. A. Barry, *Harper's Weekly* vol. 11 no. 571, 7 December 1867, p. 777

of publishing in parts. He took intense interest in how his own work could be exploited, 'working the copyrights' as he called it, by, for instance, producing different Complete Editions of his novels for different audiences, authorising theatrical versions and adapting his novels and stories for public readings. His work was extensively marketed and the success of his serials could be gauged by the pages of advertisements that accompanied them.[2] He sought audiences abroad, particularly in the US where, after a tricky start, he found outstanding success in a final reading tour (fig. 1).

He was subject to and outraged by piracy, in terms both of the unauthorised publication of his novels abroad and of the numerous unofficial adaptations generated at home; seventeen different stage versions of the Christmas story *The Cricket on the Hearth* (1845) appeared within a month of its publication and it was not uncommon for theatrical versions to be staged before the serial had even been completed.[3] He sought to control piracy, though never entirely succeeded, by making exclusive deals with foreign publishers – Harpers in New York, Hachette in Paris. He was even prepared to sacrifice artistic concerns for profitable necessity; when in 1859 a serial by another author proved unpopular and sales of his magazine declined, Dickens decided that 'the one thing to be done was, for me to strike in' by changing the planned monthly format of his next novel, *Great Expectations* (1860), to the more demanding weekly format.[4] In sum, he was 'the first professional author to *act* as a professional, and to put what could have been notable skills as a Victorian businessman to good use'.[5] And through paying such keen attention to the fact that all this was based on his own exploitation of a version of himself, he became in the process, according to a leading Dickens critic, 'what we would call today a media personality'.[6]

With a shake of the kaleidoscope, many of these concerns can be seen to be a feature of the production of modern television fiction. Serialisation has emerged as *the* characteristic television format, wiping out the early commitment to the more theatrical notion of the single play. As with Dickens, the episodic serial format can now be followed up by the complete version via a DVD box set or a download which can be watched in a different way. In exploiting his material, Dickens sought to promote 'the reproduction of his works, in innovative and multiple formats'[7] and his working of the copyright was as vigorous as that of any BBC commissioner demanding 360-degree exploitation of an initial idea. His embrace of different formats (print, theatre, dramatised readings, magazines) similarly compares with the way in which popular television programmes are from their conception open to being re-presented on-line, in print, in theatres and cinemas as well as being used in advertising or picked up in popular culture. Success abroad is the aim for many in television and particularly in the production of classic serials which have long been financed by co-production. Television executives and producers too are concerned about how piracy eats into profits and how official versions are subject to unofficial reinterpretations on YouTube. And professionals working in television are used to making changes which are driven by a concern for costs or a need to 'strike in' and rescue a floundering project. There is very little that the modern television commissioner does which is not prefigured in Dickens's energetic professional practices.

Above all the modern television executive will be concerned, as Dickens was, to establish a relationship with the audience not just with

3

regard to individual programmes but for the whole production process exemplified through a relationship with a provider (such as the BBC), a channel (like Channel 4) and/or a production company (like Endemol). This is not just a matter of audience numbers, though Dickens, like his television counterpart, measured popular success through audience figures. But in pursuit of that audience, Dickens used his magazines, Collected Editions and his readings to set up and continually reinforce a relationship with his public characterised by an intimate personal address in which he pictures himself, as well as his books, entering the private world of the home. The prefaces to his books and the editorials in the magazines aim to make a direct communication with the reader, establishing, as Michael Slater says of the preface to *Nicholas Nickleby* (1839) 'an image of himself as the intimate friend and well-loved literary companion of every individual among his phenomenal readership'.[8] The regular production of the Christmas Books and Numbers was important not just financially but as a way of entering people's homes in what he called 'a winning and immediate way'.[9] The various editions of his novels represented, in Dickens's mind, different ways of getting into the homes of his readers and staying there: thus, he tells purchasers of the Cheap Editions of his novels in 1847 that he hopes

to become, in this new guise, a permanent inmate of many English homes, where in his old shape [as a serialised work], he was only known as a guest … to be hoarded on the humble shelf where there are few books, and to lie about in libraries like any familiar piece of household stuff that is easy of replacement.[10]

Ten years later, the Library Edition appeared, aimed at 'the better class of readers who would buy them for well-furnished bookshelves'.[11] And, towards the end of his life, the Charles Dickens Edition with his signature stamped in gold upon the cover is presented by Dickens to 'the Author's countrymen' with 'his hopes that it may remain a favourite with them when he shall have left their service for ever'.[12] At his public readings, he addressed his audiences as "My good friends" and

Ackroyd's description of his first public reading suggests that 'he took to it *naturally* simply because it was natural for him to become intimate – as if "round the fire" – with seventeen hundred people'.[13] Communication was not one-way, for Dickens probably received more fan letters than any other nineteenth-century writer.[14]

The way in which Dickens established and thought about this relationship with his readers is strikingly similar to the way in which television has been characterised as developing in the twentieth century. Television has been described as the intimate screen, the equivalent of the hearth around which Dickens imagined his audiences gathering. Despite initial debates about where to put it and whether it should be on display (like the 'well-furnished bookshelves'), the television set soon became a 'familiar piece of household stuff', a routine item of furniture as well as a source of entertainment. And this domestic intimacy is extended into the way we are addressed as viewers; television speaks to the viewer directly through its presenters who wish us 'Good morning' and 'Good night' and urge us, after *Crimewatch* (BBC, 1984–) not to have nightmares. When something later deemed unsuitable is broadcast, executives apologise with the recognition that television has to be careful because it is being welcomed into people's homes. And like Dickens's fans, viewers respond as if they have a right to a say. Well before their electronically delivered comments appeared at the bottom of the screen, viewers wrote in to television and did so officially through specific programmes (such as the BBC's *Points of View* (1961–)) and unofficially to programmes, stars and characters.

This book describes some of the elements of the production of *Bleak House* (2005) which had an impact on its reception and looks at what made it distinctive as a television serial. After this introduction, Chapter 2 deals with the way it reworked some of the traditions of the classic serial and examines the publicity employed by the BBC to try to reach a new and more youthful audience. One aim of that publicity was to spin *Bleak House* as a soap opera and so Chapter 3 examines the question of serialisation and tests out that comparison with one of television's most enduring forms. Chapter 4 addresses the problem of

5

Esther, the heroine whom Dickens created as a narrator of the novel but for whom Andrew Davies, the writer of the 2005 adaptation, conceived an implacable and well-publicised dislike. The next three chapters offer an analysis of the programme itself, focusing on its narrative organisation in Chapter 5, characterisation and performance in Chapter 6 and setting in Chapter 7. In Chapter 8, I consider the serial's controversial visual organisation by looking at comments from the production team and at the reception of the programme by journalists and academic critics.

In relation to this analysis, it is worth addressing here the question of faithfulness. It is clear that watching an adaptation of *Bleak House* cannot offer the same experience as reading the novel, as the novelist Philip Hensher pointed out in an angry letter to the press,[15] and the attempt to replicate, in a different medium, every aspect of the original cannot result in a successful translation. In many cases, as I have argued elsewhere, the original source may be less important to a new version than a highly influential adaptation and viewers may well not have read the book and so be less than interested in the matter of comparison.[16] But, in writing this book, my interest in the television adaptation not only took me to the book but also to the rich critical literature on Dickens's life and writing. Because of that, I decided to make some comparisons between the novel and the adaptation and, more importantly, to draw on the history of academic commentary on the novel as a way of analysing the television version. As we shall see, the makers of *Bleak House* were acutely conscious of Dickens as the original author and saw their task as translating the energy and exuberance of his story into a modern format. John Caughie has argued that an analysis of *Bleak House* (1853) as a book and a television serial 'might allow us better to understand the literariness of literature and the visuality of television'.[17] My comparison between source and adaptation is undertaken in this spirit; it is not my intention to make fruitless judgments about how successfully the television programme reflects the book but to use the relationship between them to examine the layered and complex adaptation which is *Bleak House*.

1 The Classic Serial

The classic serial is often seen as a unique selling point for British television, and particularly for the BBC. The status and history of the classic serial on British television in many ways gave *Bleak House* (2005) its rationale but the category also presented problems. Many of the decisions taken about the programme in terms of production and publicity relate to this so this chapter offers a brief history of the development of the classic serial and the role of Dickens within it before exploring some of the key elements – public-service broadcasting, co-productions, quality drama – which can be usefully considered in relation to this genre. Finally, an account of the extensive publicity which launched *Bleak House* in the autumn of 2005 examines how the BBC tried to reposition the serial's status as a classic.

Adaptations of classics were a staple of British broadcasting before television was invented. Readings from nineteenth-century novels featured on radio in the 1920s and dramatisations became an established part of the developing schedule, for adults on Sunday evenings and for children on weekdays in separate after-school programming. Giddings and Selby note that Dickens was on television as early as July 1938, with an adaptation of the trial scene from *Pickwick Papers* (1837), but argue that the classic serial was not really initiated on television until the early 1950s with a production of Anthony Trollope's *The Warden* (1951).[18] Following this, the Sunday tea-time slot was established as a suitable time for family viewing of appropriate adaptations of the classics, including Dickens, which were 'constantly remade for television as the technology developed and the medium moved from live performance to videotape to film, from black and white to colour'.[19] The persistence of this tradition can be demonstrated by its longevity: the Sunday slot lasted until 1987. In 1964, the arrival of the second BBC channel provided a new slot on Saturday evening and in the late 1960s/1970s the BBC began to treat the classics in a 'more adult fashion ... cast[ing] around for classic literary texts which dealt seriously with socio-political issues'.[20] The 1980s represented an intense period of production for the classic serial, with significant productions from ITV such as *Brideshead Revisited* (1981), which nostalgically rendered the life of the upper classes, as well as the continuation of the darker strand offering an oblique opposition to Thatcherism. In 1995, the BBC's extraordinary success with *Pride and Prejudice* was paralleled by that of ITV's *Emma* (1995) and *Moll Flanders* (1996) – all three being written by Andrew Davies. All gave central roles to women and *Pride and Prejudice* in particular was deemed to have brought cinematic spectacle and a greater sense of freedom and play to the classic serial.

In the late 1990s, with the marketing of television overseas being seen as increasingly important for the BBC, Giddings and Selby identify a commodification of the genre with 'dramatisations of classic novels ... rapidly identified as ideal products to make at home and sell abroad'.[21] As commodities, the programmes had certain 'basic requirements':

> an authorship reasonably well known and a dramatic coherent story with good leading roles, an interesting period and offering colourful locations ... international tastes and expectations must be satisfied. A bit of expert horse trading additionally may lead to various other tie-ins.[22]

Continuing this trend, the 2000s, in the interests of sales abroad and with the possibility of overseas cinema release in mind, saw a reduction in the serial elements of the form with single-episode dramas becoming more prevalent, such as ITV's three Jane Austen adaptations in 2007 (one of which, *Northanger Abbey*, was written by Davies) and longer serials, such as Davies's adaptation of *Tipping the Velvet* (2002), came down to two or three episodes.

Throughout this history, Dickens has remained a popular source for classic adaptations. This is partly because his status as a writer with impeccable literary credentials who wrote for a popular audience has remained significant in terms of British television's obligation to fulfil its public-service broadcasting requirements. The BBC has consistently had to balance a commitment to high standards with an obligation to remain accessible to the mass public who pay a mandatory television licence. This means that it cannot retreat into a public-service niche in the way that politicians and media moguls resentful of the BBC's weight and reach sometimes demand. Dickens was significant because he combined a highly commercial approach to his audience with a commitment to the status and value of literary activity. Indeed, he resisted aristocratic patronage as the main support for literary endeavour and embraced the notion of writing for the novel-reading public rather than individual patrons. During the writing of *Bleak House*, he made a speech declaring that 'the people have set Literature free'. Any 'true man' could reach his audience, he argued, but warned against 'the coxcombical idea of writing down to the popular intelligence'.[23] This combination of a passionate interest in getting high audience numbers with a respect for the intelligence of that mass audience might be thought a good recipe for public-service broadcasting and Dickens adaptations have certainly been seen as an exemplary way of mixing the BBC's Reithian values of education and entertainment; for decades, Dickens has, according to Giddings and Selby, 'dominated the BBC classic serial tradition'.[24]

But of course British television's approach to Dickens has varied depending in part on how the Reithian vision was interpreted. Jeffrey Richards suggests that the 'Sunday teatime serial was the epitome of television as an educational, uplifting socially cohesive force'; although there had been an adaptation of *Bleak House* in 1959, the family slot generally placed the emphasis on 'Dickens the family

9

entertainer rather than Dickens the social critic' and hence screened
adaptations of the comic novels and those which had become children's
classics.[25] The shift to darker novels saw adaptations, such as *Our
Mutual Friend* (1976) and *Hard Times* (1977), based on books which
had registered less significantly on public consciousness and which
contained few of the popular figures, such as Pickwick and Fagin, who
were known to those who had never opened the books. The BBC
adaptation of *Bleak House* in 1985 fell into this category and is judged
by Giddings and Selby to be a 'significant development in the classic
serial tradition'.[26] Shot on film, directed by Ross Devenish and written
by Arthur Hopcraft, this version has been particularly praised for the
quality of its acting, the cast dropping the gurning, theatrical mode
often used for Dickens's comic grotesques and featuring actors with a
reputation for their television work such as Diana Rigg, Denholm Elliott
and Peter Vaughn. Jefferson Hunter argues that Hopcraft pared back
the language and the humour of the book in the interests of gaining a
coherent unity, to which the editing also contributed by interweaving
past and present and connecting one parallel plot action with another
visually. This led to an adaptation which was 'distinctive in a way that
involves a governing conception, a considered response to the original
but even more a steady inventiveness with small details of design, acting
and camera work'.[27] This *Bleak House* was also noted for 'an apparent
obsession with the décor and trappings of the period detail', which also
made it feel rather slow and reverent, operating at a pace only
acceptable on BBC2.[28]

Classic serials, including those based on Dickens's work, have
thus been a crucial part of British television's identity but they are costly
to produce. Giddings and Selby give the cost of *Bleak House* (1985) as
£2.8 million for an eight-hour production and BBC lore suggests that it
was too hard an act to follow. Aesthetically, according to BBC producer
Kevin Loader in 1991, this adaptation was felt to have 'elevated the level
of production so high it is impossible to follow it'; Michael Wearing, the
respected producer and BBC Head of Serials, later said that in such
period productions 'something like three-quarters of your budget goes

on design-related expenditure' and that when ITV made *Hard Times* in 1977 and the BBC responded with *Bleak House*, 'we were both bankrupting ourselves'.[29] So while classic adaptations are strongly associated with the BBC, they have long been co-productions, often with WBGH Boston, as was the case with *Bleak House*. This largely goes unpublicised to British audiences though the practice with regard to historical dramas received attention when the BBC, with HBO as the senior partner, moved into the more racy territory of *Rome* (2005–7), which was being filmed when *Bleak House* was in production.

The appeal of the classic serial is based, at least in part, on assumptions about quality. With their theatrically trained actors, period set design and high production values, classic serials were an important strand in the claim that British television was the best in the world. But increasingly, and particularly among British television critics, these elements were no longer sufficient to define quality television drama. This change had begun with the screening on Channel 4 of programmes like *Hill St Blues* (1981–7) and *E.R.* (1994–2009) but these fell within the categories of police and hospital dramas and, though enjoyable and influential with their fluid camera work and layered soundtracks, they did not challenge the notion of British television's supremacy in the field of serious drama. However, British ascendancy began to be threatened with the arrival of the HBO drama, *The Sopranos*, in 1999, which combined characteristics of the soap opera with those of the gangster film and, moreover, seemed to offer broader thematic reflections which allowed 'the disquiet of affluent life in a postmodern world lacking sincerity and shared values' to resonate throughout its six series.[30] HBO advertised itself with the slogan 'It's not TV' and its merger of serialised drama with aspects of other arts such as 'postmodern theatre or art cinema'[31] appealed to those for whom television's mass appeal was equated with dumbing down. This was television drama which could claim to be narratively absorbing, intellectually stimulating and culturally significant and it heralded what has been called a 'golden age' of US television drama. In the UK, such drama is generally shown on a minority channel (Channel 4 and its

11

sister channels, BBC2 or, from 2011, Sky Atlantic) and the acclaim for such work reached its rather absurd apogee with *The Wire* (2002–8), a programme that was screened on a minority channel and watched by very small audiences but which was nevertheless hailed as being the kind of drama no longer produced by British television.[32] The continuing frustrations about this can be seen in this comment by Jan Hunt when BBC1 channel controller:

> It does seem there's a lot of snobbery at work when the media industry spends so much time talking and writing about a handful of shows that are largely watched by people like them ... I wonder whether we are capable of having a debate about popular drama that includes other shows – shows that reach a broader audience and includes a wider part of the creative community – or whether the media will remain obsessed with *Mad Men*, *30 Rock* and *The Wire*.[33]

All of this led the BBC to fear that its equation of the classic serial with quality drama was looking old-fashioned. Its traditional pleasures – of re-presenting familiar stories and characters, of period faithfulness, of beautiful English landscapes and British acting – when combined with an air of educational worthiness, ran the risk of marooning it with a middle-class, middle-aged audience on BBC2. Laura Mackie, the BBC Head of Drama Serials, expressed something of this concern when she said, of *Bleak House*, 'we wanted to draw in an audience who might feel costume drama is a bit alienating, a bit posh'.[34] The perceived need to make a bolder stab at drama with a different storytelling approach and *mise en scène* led to programmes like *Spooks* (2002–11) but this was within the spy/thriller genre and hence lacked the educational cachet of the classic serial. Maintaining the educational aspect of BBC programming and more generally fulfilling its public-service obligations became crucial at this time, since in December 2003 the UK government had instituted a major review of the Corporation's Royal Charter and Licence. In March 2005, as *Bleak House* was being filmed, the government published its Charter Renewal Green Paper,

2. Image of *Bleak House* cast used in BBC press pack, 4 October 2005

outlining its position on some of the issues needing to be resolved in the lengthy negotiations before the planned renewal of the Charter in December 2006. It was therefore particularly important at this time that the BBC demonstrate that it was both popular with the licence-paying public and doing something different from its commercial competitors.

This background helps to explain why, as the publicity material underscored repeatedly, the BBC was 'keen to explore fresh approaches to classic adaptation'[35] (fig. 2) and why the idea of making *Bleak House* a fast-paced drama to be scheduled after its popular soap opera *EastEnders* (1985–) was appealing. The publicity for the launch of the adaptation on 4 October 2005 focuses on three main themes which indicate how the BBC wanted to position this particular classic serial. First, it emphasises Dickens himself, whose work, as we have seen, can be both educational and popular. Nigel Stafford-Clark, the producer, is quoted as saying that Dickens 'was unashamedly writing for a mainstream popular audience and that tends to get slightly forgotten today because his books have become classics'. The BBC's intention therefore, was that *Bleak House* achieve that same popularity and 'bring Dickens back to the audience for which he was writing'. Stafford-Clark goes out of his way to underline the relationship between Dickens and television and make some very specific links. 'People were excited [about his novels] in the way that they are now about a new series of a popular television drama like *Spooks* or *Shameless*', he claims, going on to rework a familiar trope about Dickens as a

13

contemporary writer: 'If Charles Dickens were alive today, he would probably be writing big signature dramas like *State of Play* or *Shameless*. He would be writing for television because he recognised a popular medium when he saw it.' Given this apparent capacity to project a nineteenth-century writer into the twenty-first century, it is hardly surprising that Stafford-Clark thinks that Dickens would '100% approve of what we've done'.

The second publicity theme ties the adaptation to the BBC's own popular-drama offering and in particular to its soaps. *Bleak House* was not the first classic serial to make a connection with soaps. With *The Forsyte Saga* (2002), ITV had set out to appeal to the youth market and its scriptwriter, Jan McVerry, had a soap background and compared the Forsyte novels to 'highbrow soap opera', with its cliff-hangers, coincidences and overlapping stories.[36] But the BBC put the force of its publicity machine behind the comparison. The press release on 19 December 2003 announcing the *Bleak House* adaptation was headlined 'Bleak House Gets the Soap Opera Treatment for BBC ONE' and quoted Laura Mackie as saying that 'The Dickens novel was very much the soap opera of its day.' When the autumn season was unveiled in the summer of 2005, Controller of BBC 1 Peter Fincham included 'a stunning reworking of Bleak House' alongside four modern-day Shakespeare adaptations, identifying them as 'big, bold pieces in a rich and varied schedule which tempt the viewers into new areas'. He continued the soap-opera theme by adding that 'It's the role of BBC ONE to take risks, whether that is commissioning ... Shakespeare adaptations to deliver the classics in a new and unusual way, or scheduling the forerunners of the soaps in a way that modern audiences understand.'[37] A press release on 16 September 2005, promoting the first episode, connected it to the BBC soaps *Casualty* (1986–) and *EastEnders* and promised that all three would make up 'a dramatic week of exciting programmes'.

But there is some ambivalence about this association and considerable variation in the way in which soap opera is invoked by those involved in the programme. Initially the emphasis is on its

scheduling in thirty-minute episodes after *EastEnders* and thus
hopefully ensnaring a new audience.[38] In the press pack, writer Davies
expresses the BBC's hopes that the scheduling will 'catch a slightly
different and broader audience than usual … . It's early enough for older
primary school children to watch' while Stafford-Clark seeks to
generate the type of audience anticipation created by a programme like
the US *24* (2001–10): 'You get that feeling of: "Is it over already? I want
to see the next episode!" That's exactly what we want, because with
this the pace of it is fast and more akin to a contemporary show'.[39] But
Davies is consistent and upfront in using the soap analogy in interviews,
with comments like 'If Dickens was alive today, he'd be writing for
EastEnders'[40] and 'I deliberately tried to make it, in some ways, like a
soap.'[41] Among the actors, Denis Lawson, who plays John Jarndyce,
also adopts the soap analogy in a publicity interview included in the
press pack: '*Bleak House* is like the best soap you could ever hope to
watch. It has the same structure as *EastEnders*, in half hours, and the
characters are so rich. The narrative twists and turns are just fantastic.'
But American Gillian Anderson, who plays Lady Dedlock, cites a
different television term, observing that 'Appointment television,
something that people make sure they never miss … has become very
popular over the last ten years.' This term and her timescale connect the
adaptation to US drama rather than British soaps.

      The third theme in the publicity is the emphasis on advanced
technology and a modern approach to the drama. Anderson suggests
that 'Even though it is not set in a contemporary setting, there is
something contemporary about the way it is shot – it's filmed in HD and
it's in a half hour format' and Lawson, who had not been in a period
television drama before, stresses this paradox: 'It's also been shot in a
very contemporary style, so it's going to feel like a really modern bit of
television – but look period.' Stafford-Clark's 'production diary', made
available to viewers as part of the publicity, mentions that they were
filming on High Definition tape which 'everyone said was the medium
of the future. All the major US TV dramas were moving onto it.'
Stafford-Clark uses this to suggest that far from this period drama being

familiar territory for the BBC, and the audience, HD makes the whole thing new: 'No-one had used it for a period show, and no-one knew how it would work.'[42]

We will return to these issues in subsequent chapters but should note here that the BBC's focus on Dickens as a popular writer and on soap opera as a format succeeded in shaping the press response. The press office got its headlines – 'BLEAKENDERS' from the *Manchester Evening News*, 'Dickens with cliffhangers' from London's *Evening Standard*, 'The BBC's new cockney soap' in the *Guardian* and 'What the Dickens! BBC Rebuilds "Bleak House" for the "Hollyoaks" Generation', in the *Independent*.[43] More importantly for the audience which the BBC was trying to attract, the *Sun* and the *Mirror* provided glossy guides and the television weeklies, afforded the adaptation soap-style commentaries on a day-by-day basis with updates like 'After last night's astonishing confession Esther is trying to pull herself together ... . Beautiful performances are the making of this moving instalment – keep the tissues handy' and 'There's an unwritten rule in soap that shattering episodes start quietly, and so it is here.'[44]

However, the BBC hype about soap scheduling may have raised aspirations about viewing figures which were impossible to fulfil. The hour-long first episode on 27 October got an audience of 7.32 million, which put it above ITV's long-running police series *The Bill* (1984–2010) and the BBC's own popular series *Spooks*, which Stafford-Clark had cited as one of his production benchmarks. This was a very respectable 30.82 per cent share and the first two episodes were third and fourth in *Broadcast*'s drama top ten for the week on 30 October, a top ten which does not include soaps. The Friday 8.30 pm episode was consistently weaker than Thursday's 8 pm slot and viewing figures dropped down to 5.66 million (23.81 per cent share) in the week ending 20 November. But figures picked up again and the week ending 27 November saw both episodes back in the drama top ten with the Friday episode getting 6.12 million (28.57 per cent share).[45] As could be expected, therefore, *Bleak House* did hold on to some of the *EastEnders* audience but its figures were also affected by what ITV was putting up alongside it. Nevertheless, rather than judging success against *EastEnders* figures, it might be better to compare it to *The Bill*, then a consistent performer for ITV in the 8–9 pm slot, and suggest that keeping *The Bill* in sight and occasionally beating it was a commendable performance for a classic serial operating outside its comfort zone.

   Bleak House was on more familiar ground at award ceremonies. In the UK, the serial took awards at BAFTA and Royal Television Society ceremonies in 2006, winning the Best Drama Serial at both events. Among other awards at BAFTA, Anna Maxwell Martin won Best Actress and at the RTS Andrew Davies was voted Best Writer. At the Broadcasting Press Guild Awards, *Bleak House* was named Best Drama Series, Gillian Anderson won Best Actress and Charles Dance Best Actor (triumphing over both Christopher Eccleston and David Tennant as the two new Doctor Whos). In the US, at the 2006 Emmys, the programme was nominated for ten awards and won two: Outstanding Cinematography for a Miniseries or Movie for Kieran McGuigan as Director of Photography and Outstanding Makeup for a Miniseries, Movie or a Special (Non-prosthetic) which went to Daniel Phillips as Makeup Department Head. In 2007, it was nominated for two Golden Globes (Best Mini-Series or Motion Picture Made for Television and Best Performance by an Actress in the same category for Gillian Anderson). Overall it won eighteen awards out of twenty-nine nominations.[46]

   Given the ambitions of this production, the press response, audience figures and professional accolades can be said to have made *Bleak House* a success for the BBC, both at home and in terms of international sales. Certainly the programme was used as evidence of the successful fulfilment of its public-service remit during the Charter Renewal process. Two examples of this appear in carefully positioned speeches by senior BBC figures in 2006. Peter Fincham, at the annual spring conference of the lobbying organisation, the Voice of the Listener and Viewer, in April referred to *Bleak House* as an example of the BBC at its best:

17

> Occasionally, on BBC ONE, all the qualities that we're looking for come together at once in a programme or series that stands testament to what the BBC is for. It happened last autumn with our dramatisation of Dickens's *Bleak House*.[47]

And just a day earlier, on 25 April 2006, Mark Thompson, the BBC Controller, gave the annual Royal Television Society Fleming Memorial Lecture and emphasised that, in all the technical debates about BBC governance and accountability, 'the point of the BBC is its content'. Part of that content was *Bleak House* and the company it kept in Thompson's speech emphasised the BBC's intentions concerning new drama: 'We're taking more commissioning and scheduling risks on BBC ONE – *Bleak House*, Shakespeare, *Doctor Who*. Drama is stronger and livelier today than it's been for years.'[48]

2 Serialisation and Soaps

We have seen that the BBC pitched this version of *Bleak House* by making a specific comparison between Dickens's mode of serialisation and the production of soap operas such as its own *EastEnders*. The notion that Dickens, were he alive today, would be writing for television is not a new one; novelist David Lodge and biographer Claire Tomalin, for instance, proposed variations on the idea in a 1994 television programme about Dickens.[49] For many Dickens scholars, though, the idea is crassly a-historical and, when Robert Giddings rhetorically asked 'Can this Dickens/soap opera thing be taken seriously?', he quickly concluded that 'the assertion that Dickens's novels are soap operas and that nowadays he'd be writing TV soaps is flippant'.[50] Nevertheless, it seems to me that the comparisons between Dickens's mode of writing serial fiction and the production and textual features of soap opera are worthy of analysis, if only to temper the looser versions of such claims. This chapter then will look at Dickens's writing practices and publishing serially, with the aim of comparing them with those of television serials and soap operas. In doing so, it will open up areas to be explored further in the more detailed analysis of later chapters.

Grahame Smith makes the point that Dickens wrote serial fiction rather than fiction that was then divided up for serial publication.[51] This meant that he was continually up against deadlines; that in the early days, he began stories without necessarily knowing how they were going to end; that he had to write to length; and that he shifted between formats depending on whether he was writing weekly or monthly episodes. For a monthly publication like *Bleak House*, there would be nineteen monthly numbers consisting of three or four chapters, with the last number a double issue wrapping up the novel. Serials tended to start in the spring and fictional seasons would to some extent match the time of publication.[52] Dickens wrote about social issues of the day – poverty, disease, homelessness, class relations – and sought to emphasise the topicality and accuracy of his stories; hence, for instance, his explanation of the science of Krook's spontaneous combustion in his preface to *Bleak House* and his insistence that the critique of Chancery was still pertinent in the 1850s.[53] According to Butt and Tillotson, Dickens never wrote more than four or five numbers ahead of publication and, by the middle of a novel, 'he was rarely more than one number ahead of his readers'.[54] Dickens would start writing in the first week of the month, with the aim of submitting the full text on the twentieth of the month, by which time he would also have given detailed instructions for the two illustrations which generally accompanied each number. He knew how much he had to write to meet the quota of thirty-two printed pages for each month though he regularly consulted his printers about how to remedy problems of 'over-writing', when he had written too much or, more seriously, when he came in under length, as he did on one occasion with *Bleak House* number XVI.[55] As he wrote to Wilkie Collins, his friend and fellow writer, 'I was stricken ill when I was doing *Bleak House*, and I shall not easily forget what I suffered under the fear of not being able to come up to time'.[56] While the rhythms of this monthly publishing routine were demanding enough, they were hardly to be compared to the rigours of writing for weekly publication. Dickens declared that writing *Hard Times* (1854) in weekly parts after *Bleak House* was 'CRUSHING' and later wrote of *Great Expectations* that 'as to the planning out from week to week, nobody can imagine what the difficulty is, without trying' but added that 'when it is overcome, the pleasure is proportionate'.[57] The pleasure and terror of the situation are neatly summed up in one anecdote in which Dickens recalls overhearing a lady in the stationers shop ask for 'the new green number', and realised that she wanted the next number of *David Copperfield* (1850) and remembering that 'not one word of the number she was asking for was yet written'.[58]

The pressures of writing for serial publication had an impact on how Dickens wrote and the kind of texts he produced but this changed as Dickens developed as a writer and publisher. In particular, he learnt how to control the potential openness of the serial with the need to plan a complex story which could be written and read over a long period of time and to develop characters who would remain vivid and memorable within such plots. This kind of serial publishing could be expected to generate loose, picaresque storytelling and the early novels do share a somewhat meandering course, with the story emerging as a series of adventures linked by the central character as in *The Pickwick Papers* and *Oliver Twist* (1839). But by the time of *Bleak House*, Dickens was working with a double focus, planning his novels so that they worked as serial fiction and later as a coherent novel; he 'had to think in terms of the identity of the serial number, which would have to make its own impact and be judged as a unit' (Butt and Tillotson, 1957, p. 15) but he also had to work to an overall design for the novel to be published afterwards. Memoranda or 'mems' have survived which point to some of his methods for maintaining control of ideas and planning the overall story. They operated both 'as a structural key and as an aide-memoire'.[59] On the lefthand page, Dickens makes notes of ideas, names, themes that he wants to remember and weave into the story; on the righthand page, the numbers and chapters are broken down into the main incidents and events, sometimes written as if roughing out the direction the chapter will take, and emphasising salient points, and sometimes jotted down after the writing has been completed, to act as a reminder of the content needed to carry the story forward in the next number.[60] Slater notes that 'Dickens's "mems" for *Bleak House* show him looking far ahead to later plot developments' and those for the final number include what looks like a checklist of events and characters with ticks added against their names to indicate that they have been dealt with in some way.[61]

21

One further aspect of the serialisation process is the tendency for it to drive towards collaboration. While Dickens valued the tight control he held over his work as writer, editor and publisher, the pressures of writing serially necessarily involved trusting others at key points; and Smith suggests that he enjoyed acting as a conductor, bringing big projects, including magazine issues and theatre productions, in together and on time. The illustrations were a key feature of each number but work on them could not wait for Dickens to finish writing. He would make recommendations for subjects, offer detailed suggestions and would generally see a proof for final approval but he had to rely on his illustrator's ideas and skills. In the case of *Bleak House*, the illustrator was Hablot K. Browne who, under the name 'Phiz', illustrated most of Dickens's novels up to *Little Dorrit* (1857). Smith also points to the role of John Forster, Dickens's friend, manager and first biographer, who, in taking responsibility for the proofs, had a 'great deal of leeway to cut and revise'.[62] And Dickens also adopted highly collaborative practices as an editor, going so far as to suggest, rather wickedly, to one valued contributor, a sick Wilkie Collins, that he himself would keep the publication of the serialised novel *No Name* (1862) going, by writing it 'so like you as that no one would find out the difference'.[63]

The serial form created 'an especially intimate and fluctuating relationship between Dickens and his readers',[64] which engendered much excitement at various stages in the publishing process. Big sales were the norm on the first day; *Bleak House*'s initial print run of 25,000 sold out within three days in February 1852 and each month the streets were full of fluttering bluish-green covers as the new number went on sale.[65] Public interest would heighten at key points in the story so that Dickens, for instance, recorded, as he wrote *The Old Curiosity Shop* in 1840, that 'I am inundated with imploring letters recommending poor little Nell to mercy'.[66] But the main aim was to maintain a consistent interest throughout, 'keeping up the desire to ascertain what it is about through every successive number' as the *Illustrated London News* reported that Dickens had achieved with

A Tale of Two Cities in 1859. The ending could generate fevered discussion and review. According to the *Illustrated London News*, 'What do you think of *Bleak House*?' was a question that 'everybody had heard propounded within the last few weeks' as the final number came out in September 1853.[67] But there could also be sadness without the anticipation of more instalments, as a contemporary review of *Dombey and Son* (1848) vividly illustrated:

> Those … who have like ourselves, discovered the work bit by bit – familiarizing themselves by long association with the every characteristic of the ideal personages depicted in the narrative … will comprehend our regret at the dispersion of this imaginary multitude [of characters].[68]

But though hugely successful, there was contemporary criticism of the serialised format and intimations that it made Dickens too dependent on his readers. The *Spectator* noted, as *Bleak House* reached its end in September 1853, that Dickens's 'peculiar genius and his method of exhibiting it' meant that author and public reacted to each other in a powerful way; this success made Dickens 'deaf to the remonstrances of critics when they warn him of defects that his public does not care for' and made him 'content with amusing the idle hours of the greatest number of readers'.[69] An earlier review of *David Copperfield* asserted that 'the serial form … is probably the lowest artistic form yet invented' and suggested that 'nine tenths of its readers will never look at it or think of it as a whole', deeming that it was destined only for amusing 'the lounger in the coffee room or the traveller by the railway'.[70] Dickens too sometimes had his doubts, regretting for instance that the final third of *Great Expectations*, then being published weekly, could not be read 'all at once … because its purpose would be much more apparent'.[71]

Much of this criticism, including the accusations of pandering to a popular audience, would be familiar territory to those making soap operas, as the impact of the practices engendered by serialisation has intensified with the continuing industrialisation of the process in

23

television. Episodes of a soap opera are written to a set length and normally involve a number of interweaving storylines in order to ensure that a variety of its highly recognisable characters is covered in a week's episodes. Soaps recognise the seasons and the passing of time experienced by the audience in, for instance, episodes which use Christmas or summer holidays as the background for stories. Stories take up topical themes which reflect the social issues of the day – child neglect or abuse, racial or gender prejudices, mental illness, unemployment – and producers and writers defend the accuracy of their controversial storylines by pointing to what happens in the real world. Soaps employ suspense to maintain their audiences' interest in between episodes and episodes are carefully constructed to encourage the audience to return.

It was this engagement with suspense, which they saw in both Dickens and soap opera, that was, according to the publicity, the key feature of serialisation for the production team of *Bleak House*. The BBC Head of Drama, Jane Tranter wanted 'a sense of energy given by the cliffhanger endings and a narrative of real velocity' and felt that they had got 'something that feels absolutely authentic' to Dickens's use of instalments.[72] In the press pack, Stafford-Clark emphasised that Dickens 'was absolutely tuned in to the needs of an audience so he wrote for serialisation; he used cliff-hangers as a way of getting an audience to come back for the next episode'; Davies similarly was caught up in the importance of creating suspense: 'the thing that was uppermost in our minds was to tell the story in a way that made people absolutely die to know what happens next'. I will comment shortly on how soaps handle suspense but we need to be aware that Dickens was more subtle than these comments might imply; he 'did not, as is sometimes supposed, use serial publication in the interest of crude suspense' and would sometimes end a number with a chapter which 'subdues the drama'.[73] And, of course, since the television *Bleak House* was an adaptation, the ending was actually already known by at least some of the audience. In placing such a stress on suspense and 'what happened next', the producer and writer were in tune with the BBC strategy of seeking to attract a popular audience unfamiliar with the book and thus of valuing one kind of audience over another.

Like Dickens, soap-opera writers have to operate with a double focus, with each episode needing to work as a topical and engaging instalment but also to contribute to a much longer and larger story, which is generally planned months and years in advance. When the Slater family, with its five daughters, was introduced to *EastEnders* in September 2000, the planning for their stories was extensive, including the revelations about abuse and incest which were to emerge over a year later when teenage Zoe (Michelle Ryan) discovered that her sister Kat (Jessie Wallace) was in fact her mother. Like Dickens, soap-opera producers value their relationship with their audiences and take their wishes into account but, also like Dickens, who killed off both Little Nell and young Paul Dombey, they cannot generally allow audiences to determine the specifics of what will happen next; in 2011, the decision to curtail an *EastEnders*' storyline about baby stealing generated publicity because it was so unusual for a soap to deviate from its long-term plans.[74] This planning requires disciplined collaboration, led by the executive producer, with stories mapped out by a central team, including key writers, while story editors will inform the writers of individual episodes which storylines must be carried forward either as main events or as references to plot events to come. Everyone working on a soap, including the actors, has to work to a deadline, meaning that the process can easily become a mechanical treadmill, one that is driven by the commitment to the waiting audience.[75]

The publicity for *Bleak House* drew attention to the pressures and compromises of the production schedules, claiming these to be similar to those experienced by Dickens and by those working on a soap opera, although the *Bleak House* production team was not actually following the week-by-week timetable of a soap. Stafford-Clark's production diary gives what was clearly felt to be valuable publicity to such stories. He reports, for instance, that his 'skin went clammy' (a fine Dickensian touch) when he was told that the transmission date had been brought forward by three months just as shooting started. There were

25

problems with under-writing when they realised the material would not last for twenty episodes and they had to drop to fewer episodes while one episode was over-length and had to be restructured in shooting.[76] The very large cast (forty principals and 2,000 extras) was comparable to that of a soap, with some more or less permanent players and others only there for a day or two. According to Stafford-Clark's diary, preparing the shooting schedule with such numbers felt, like 'playing three-dimensional chess'.

In an interview promoting the finished serial, Stafford-Clark emphasised the pace of the twenty-one-week shoot, pointing out that his team was making an hour's television in thirteen days compared to the sixteen/seventeen days more usual with classic serials.[77] The consequences of this were noted in the production diary: at the finish of a demanding day's work, 'the call sheet which detailed the next day's shooting would be thrust into our hands, and we would look at each other in disbelief'. There was a change of director after thirteen weeks and the incoming director, Susanna White, described joining a production working at this pace as like getting aboard a fast train. And some things were just very difficult to get 'right' in the time available. They managed to film Miss Flite's (Pauline Collins) birds despite the practical problems of conforming with animal-welfare regulations and the televisual problems of maintaining continuity as the birds flew about. But an exterior shot showing the ships at Deal was too expensive to contemplate and, as we shall see, filming *Bleak House*'s fog was an intractable problem, despite some attempts to add it at the post-production stage.[78]

The publicity material also stresses collaboration as being a feature of the production set-up. In the production diary, Stafford-Clark describes the 'relentlessness' of the writing regime and clearly places Davies, as the named writer, in the production process. Early on, Stafford-Clark realises that Davies, like Dickens, will have to work very quickly:

> When I worked the schedule backwards I realised that Andrew would have to write two episodes a month for ten months. And his first drafts would

have to be pretty close to perfect, because all the revisions would have to be fitted into the same period.

But the writing process was designed to make this possible and bears comparison, in its use of the producer and script editor, with soap practices. The production diary records how Stafford-Clark and the initial script editor, Ellie Wood, broke the book down into twenty parts; after getting Davies's initial ideas on each episode, they would work on a detailed storyline which Davies would review; 'when he was happy he'd start to write, while we made notes on the episode he'd just delivered'. None of this is particularly unusual in the production of popular television drama but, in terms of the production of a classic serial, this emphasis on the pressure to deliver on time, and hence the need for collaboration, should temper the tendency to treat Davies as the sole author.

Anyone working on a soap would consider that the *Bleak House* team was let off lightly, in that the whole production and transmission process stopped after less than two years. But there is something here, in the way in which the production stories are told, which reflects the feelings which the creation of a long, serialised work engenders. White's analogy that joining the production was akin to boarding a fast-moving train is an apt one, both in terms of its Dickensian flavour and its industrial connotations, in which human beings are driven to work at the pace of a machine. Serialisation as a process commits creators to an industrial pace of work, driven by (magazine or television) schedules, but one in which the pressure can produce creative possibilities and audience engagement.

Taking all this into account, it seems to me that there are connections between the emphasis on serial narrative in both novel and adaptation and the practices of soap opera. The reviewer who mourned the end of *Dombey and Son*, as we saw earlier, referred to reading practices which are recognisable in soap viewers, who also may have 'discovered the work bit by bit – familiarizing themselves by long association with the every characteristic of the ideal personages depicted

27

in the narrative'. And the *Spectator*'s comment as *Bleak House* reached
its end in 1853 that 'Old Jarndyce himself, too, is so dreadfully amiable
and supernaturally benevolent that it has been a common opinion
during the progress of the book, that he would turn out as great a rascal
as Skimpole'[79] exactly captures the kind of discussion about character,
based on knowledge of the serial form as well as moral principles,
familiar to a soap viewer.

Nevertheless, the soap-opera comparison does not fit as
neatly as the BBC publicity implied and, to some extent, rests on a
misunderstanding about the use and function of suspense and the effect
of an ending. *Bleak House*, as a novel and as an adaptation, finishes
with most of its loose ends resolved. It can do this because its characters
(even down to its minor figures) are there because they relate in some
way to the central story and the viewing process is premised on the
promise of a denouement. But a soap is organised differently. While an
episode or series of episodes may share a theme, often with serious and
comic variations of a particular situation, no overall story, however
capacious, can hold all the characters. A soap never reaches a final
conclusion and soaps which are cancelled and come to an end have to
stop in full flow, leaving characters dangling and stories unfinished.
That is because the unity of a soap is based not on key stories climaxing
together, as in *Bleak House*, but on the organisation of space. Soaps take
place in a particular location (the Square, the Street, the Hospital) which
allows characters and stories to come and go while retaining the
programme's distinctive identity. The endless nature of soap storytelling
means that the soap-opera appeal is rooted not just in the suspense
generated by exciting stories but in the anticipation of stories as yet
unwritten to unfold in this place.

The organisation of time in soaps is also different, taking
on the rhythm of daily life, with unrecorded time passing between
episodes, which in *EastEnders* often start afresh with characters
getting ready for a new day. This affects the creation of suspense since
episodes, while they close on a compelling question, rarely answer it in
the classic cliff-hanger manner by returning to the same point in the

storyline. Stafford-Clark and Davies aim to create sufficient suspense to compel the viewer of *Bleak House* to watch every episode in order to follow the strong narrative connections. Missing an episode hinders understanding, thus threatening the viewer's pleasure in the story. But the soap viewer, faced with up to five episodes a week over many decades, has to be given more leeway. Over many years (the British soap *Coronation Street* has been running since 1960 and *EastEnders* since 1985), the successful soap builds up a history of past events which is known to such varying degrees by individual viewers that knowledge of it cannot be routinely assumed in current stories. It has to be possible to drop in and out of a soap narrative, to recognise the character types and catch up on stories without requiring the detailed knowledge necessary to follow a finite text leading to a definitive ending. And while narrative action is important in soaps, so too is talk, since very often the dilemma posed is a moral one; suspense depends not on 'what will happen next?' but 'what judgment should we make about what has happened?'. Talk between the characters and indeed within the audience will often fill out the narrative by pointing up the social and moral dilemmas of the story. Action in the storyline has to be balanced against reflection and comment; soaps build in moments of resolution and rest to set against the action.

29

We will pick up on issues arising out of serialisation and suspense in *Bleak House* in later chapters on narrative organisation, location and characterisation but one further element requires discussion here and that is the question of melodrama. The term, 'melodrama' is frequently set against realism and in that binary is regularly used to draw attention to problematic elements in both Dickens's work and soap operas. In such criticism, melodrama is associated with an excessive sentimentality and a readiness to fulfil the demand of the popular audience for emotional satisfaction but it is important to put it in a broader context which allows us to see melodrama as an aesthetic mode of interpreting the world. If realism offers a way of analysing how society works, both on the surface (in terms of naturalism) and in terms of its inner drives and forces, then melodrama can be understood as recognition of what it feels like to be at the mercy of those forces and an attempt to identity moral responsibility for their operation. Juliet John argues that Dickens's work 'functions as a bridge between the most popular form of entertainment in his day (stage melodrama) and the most popular form of entertainment in the age that followed (the screen)'.[80] Dickens's novels meet soap opera in working in this melodramatic field and, while the identification of good and evil can be rendered too simplistically and the workings of the plot become too mechanical, melodrama is embraced for the way in which it forces attention to the dilemmas of personal life into any scrutiny of public institutions and gives voice to those at the bottom of the social pile – young men, women and children in particular. When Smith in 1968 suggested that, in *Bleak House*, the focus on the Chancery allowed Dickens to bring the themes of earlier books 'from the private into the public sphere,'[81] he was using terms which feminist criticism in the 1980s would make central to an understanding of melodrama as it operated in television soap opera.

30

This emphasis on melodrama may be considered inappropriate in two ways. First, for some it may seem to emphasise the worst of Dickens, the entertainer rather than the social reformer, the creator of exaggerated types rather than realistic characters and situations. Smith's early discussion of *Bleak House* suggests that the story of Tulkinghorn's pursuit of Lady Dedlock lacks motivation and psychological realism, drawing on 'the very cheapest of melodramatic devices'.[82] It would also seem that the *Bleak House* adaptors, while willing to embrace the serialisation processes of soap opera, were wary of slipping into melodrama. Thus, in the DVD commentary on the death of Jo, Stafford-Clark comments that 'in the book, the scene is quite melodramatic' but he and White, the director, express their concern to 'get the level of it natural' and to keep it 'real'.[83]

A second objection to covering melodrama in this discussion might reference the fact that British soap operas are often assigned to the realist end of the soap-opera spectrum and deemed to be operating within the generic boundaries of social realism. But this is to underestimate how much British soaps have changed in the last ten years. While *Coronation Street* and *EastEnders* retain their commitment to the representation of working-class life, communal values and everyday storylines which stress stoicism and survival, they also feature stories which emphasise extremes of good and evil and focus on characters, particularly women, who are isolated from their community. Female characters, far from being the strong matriarchs traditionally associated with soaps, are regularly presented as victims in stories involving violence and abuse. The more traditional realist mode entailing the representation of everyday streets and recognisable, often humorous, characters now runs alongside stories which are handled melodramatically, with a shift to the use of symbolic and often dangerous locations outside the familiar setting, a different style attempting to render visually the moral dilemmas posed and a heightened manner of performance.[84]

 This discussion of serialisation and melodrama gives us some specific issues to consider when looking at the television adaptation of *Bleak House*. These include aspects of serialisation which the adaptation team thought important, in particular its impact on the organisation of the narrative, the use of cliff-hangers and the handling of characters as well as less obvious issues around the organisation of space and setting. In addition, positioning these issues in the broader context of soap opera and melodrama opens up questions of gender and the interaction between public institutions and the private sphere of the home. These will be pertinent issues as we look next at the handling of the heroine of the book and the serial, Esther Summerson (Anna Maxwell Martin).

3 The Problem of Esther

As the heroine of the novel (see fig. 3), Esther will be important for our discussion of narration and characterisation; she provided the narrative voice for half the novel and, it has been argued, presented an account which is suffused with feminine (soap) values and dominated by private issues of birth, love and marriage as opposed to the public world of Chancery. But Esther was also consistently identified as a problem by Andrew Davies who describes her character as one of his main difficulties with the novel. This chapter will look at what it was about this heroine which generated such a strong reaction and what that tells us about the heroine of the classic serial.

Davies expressed his dislike of Esther forcibly in a number of interviews he gave to academics interested in the adaptation process. In October 2004, while the script was being written, he commented to Deborah Cartmell and Imelda Whelehan that Dickens's heroines were 'dismayingly soppy and unrealized' and said that he had dropped Esther's 'smugness, all her toe-curling nicknames'. He reiterated this view to Robert Giddings in December 2004, when he said that 'to most modern readers, Esther's self-regarding, coy and disingenuous presentation of self is distinctly off-putting'. In a public interview at De Montfort University in February 2005, he spoke of the pleasure he took in abandoning Esther's 'smug and self-regarding' narration and condemns the character as 'a bore and a prig' unlikely to appeal to the modern young audience targeted by the the BBC. Years after working on the serial, he expressed himself even more

3. Esther on arrival in London

strongly declaring Esther to be 'one of the most repellent characters in English Literature'.[85]

   Davies himself seems to suggest that Esther's characterisation poses a particular problem for modern audiences, mentioning to a *Sunday Times* journalist that 'my first audience tends to be strong-minded, stroppy women – those are the people who run BBC drama – and they like to see characters like themselves'.[86] It is also the case that Esther's characterisation runs against that of the typical heroine of the classic serial, which of course Davies himself had played a major part in creating in the 1990s/2000s. Sarah Cardwell, writing about Davies's work up until 2002, comments on his liking for 'strong female protagonists' who frequently 'play the roles the world wishes them to play, while retaining a sense of self-identity behind these performances'.[87] If *Pride and Prejudice* springs to mind here, it is hardly surprising, but in the context of Esther Summerson it is worth noting the fundamentally anachronistic nature of heroines like Elizabeth Bennet, Becky Sharp and Eleanor Dashwood as they have been adapted for film and television by Davies, Emma Thompson and others. Largely eschewing the intensity of melodrama, these adaptations have been built up around the romance narrative, allowing the heroine to drive dramas whose appeal is based on their articulation of 'gender difference and female desire'.[88] In order for this to work, the heroine has (as Davies feared would not be the case with Esther) to be easy to identify with. Julianne Pidduck suggests that such adaptations share 'a pervasive liberal feminist discourse that constructs an international Western, female audience'.[89] This sensibility feels the discrimination of patriarchal laws and the unfairness of the restricted lives of women while at the same time enjoying seeing the heroine pushing against the boundaries of female mobility and gazing at her objects of desire (which in the case of Elizabeth Bennet (Jennifer Ehle) in Davies's adaptation are both Pemberley and Colin Firth's Darcy). This leads to the situation identified by Kamilla Elliott, in which adaptations attempt to be faithful to nineteenth-century furniture and décor but 'reject and correct Victorian psychology, ethics and politics' and more particularly incorporate modern ways of understanding and expressing love.[90] Thus, the updating of the adaptation is not 'in the realm of issues but of emotions'; 'the language of passion is injected into the story … on the assumption that it had been latently there all the time'.[91] Political issues of freedom and equality are translated into a romantic situation in which equality can be achieved, repressions worked through and love finally spoken of.

It is clear that the character of Esther does not readily fit this scenario (though Dickens does make some effort to make Allan Woodcourt a romantic hero) but what is not clear, from Davies's assertion that she would not work for a modern (female) audience, is that Esther had caused problems right from the start in 1852–3. The reviewer in the *Athenaeum* found her in 'her surpassingly sweet way' to be as unrealistic as Krook and Skimpole.[92] The *Spectator* found her 'a coarse portraiture, but utterly untrue and inconsistent', adding that 'such a girl would not write her own memoirs, and certainly would not bore one with her goodness'.[93] *Bentley's Miscellany*, tongue in cheek, suggested that 'a little more strength of character would not be objectionable – even in a wife'.[94] *Blackwood's Edinburgh Magazine* objected that 'in her extreme consciousness, Esther is too conscious by half' and, much like Davies, described her as 'simpering with a wearisome sweetness'.[95] And even the reviewer for *Puttnam's Magazine* who found Esther to be 'gentle, loving, true-hearted and womanly' nevertheless also commented that, in terms of her as a narrator, 'her picture of herself is an unnatural contrivance'.[96] Even John Forster, commented on 'the too conscious unconsciousness of Esther' and declared that her narrative was, by comparison with David Copperfield's storytelling in Dickens's previous novel, over-ingenious and artificial.[97] So the problem of Esther is not so much that she is too old-fashioned and Victorian for a modern audience. She has in fact been a problem all along.

After this start, the characterisation of Esther has been the subject of extensive and continuing debate in critical commentary on Dickens's work. Some of the criticism is within the boundary of what one might think of as normal critical disagreement. A. E. Dyson describes her as 'the most intelligent good woman that Dickens drew' but argues that she is unpopular as a character now because of changing attitudes to 'humility and gratitude'. Where 'a modern Esther might brood on the problem of her identity', Dickens's creation endures her suffering and seeks to spread 'sanity and healing'.[98] But, like Davies, a number of male critics have expressed their views forcefully and indeed, some of these are striking in their determination to declare that Esther does not (should not, cannot) exist. Vladimir Nabokov suggested in the 1950s that 'it was a mistake to let Esther tell part of the story. I would not have let the girl near.'[99] Robert Garis claimed that no one had ever thought Esther a successful character, arguing that 'she is empty', 'has no convincing inner life' and 'has no will, no sense of ego, hardly an identity at all'.[100] Terms like 'ego' and 'identity' suggest that modern concepts of personality are being applied here but other commentators go further and suggest that she has no bodily existence. So John Carey argued that 'Esther Summerson's smallpox means nothing to us because, as far as we are concerned, she had no face' and Angus Wilson declared in 1962 that the smallpox plot device was ineffective since 'she has no body upon which a head could rest'.[101] One could of course argue that no fictional character has a real body (unless loaned it by an actor in an adaptation) but such a denial of Esther's is indicative of the intense hostility Esther has aroused in critics other than Davies.

Nevertheless, Esther has her defenders and, as Jeremy Hawthorn implied, it is probably not an accident 'that women critics have, generally, a more positive view of Esther'.[102] While approaches differ, they are interesting for my purposes because they take up issues which would fall very much within the terrain of soap opera – such as illegitimacy, the loss of a mother, the creation of an alternative family and child abuse. Q. D. Leavis in 1970 claimed that Dickens was 'a pioneer' who took the novel 'into the realm of psychological truth in depth'.[103] She suggests that Esther is 'a very carefully complete study of what a sensitive child is made into' by the circumstances of her birth and her early repressive upbringing. She argues that this start in life is responsible for many of the traits for which Esther is maligned: the craving for affection that she does not believe she is worthy of; the confusion over what she feels and what she is told to feel; the renunciation of her own feelings which is compensated for by the mothering she bestows on others. Leavis insists on the importance of Esther to the novel and suggests that she 'has been consistently under-rated by critics'.[104]

In 1974, Grahame Smith, himself giving a sensitive account of Esther's characterisation, could describe Leavis as 'a rare exception', while the majority of critics assumed that 'Esther was to be taken quite straight-forwardly as an uncomplicated picture of domestic virtue'.[105] But the critical consensus has shifted in thirty years and now much more commonly views Esther as a woman robbed of her sense of self who, in her narration, embarks on 'rewriting the unsatisfactory tale of her birth and childhood'.[106] Virginia Blain argues that Esther has adopted the patriarchal values of her society (which tell her that it would have been better if she had not been born) and that her 'own selfhood is very much in question as a result'. Marked by the sexual stigma inherited from her mother, she is willing to sacrifice her sexuality for her 'father', John Jarndyce.[107] Alex Zederling argues that the book records the impact of a childhood trauma, 'a wound that never fully heals', outlining its 'long-range effects and the stages of an attempt to triumph over it'. He sums up the characterisation of Esther as achieving 'a subtle psychological portrait clear in its outline and convincing in its details' though he finds the ending a fantasy.[108] Anny Sadrin sees more development in Esther, arguing that Esther gradually becomes the heroine of her own story and earns 'the possibility of existing as a woman in her own right'.[109] So prevalent has this reading of Esther become that, in 2004, a year before the BBC version was transmitted, the editor of a textbook on *Bleak House* can, without equivocation, introduce it as a great book which combines 'a sustained attack on several of the most pressing issues of the day with a moving account of Esther Summerson's search for origins and selfhood'.[110]

What is interesting for me here is not so much the different details of these accounts of Esther's characterisation but that Davies makes no reference to this critical debate in trying to come to terms with the problem as he identifies it. There are hints that Davies could have taken a route which would have led to a more sympathetic approach to Esther. In his conversation with Cartmell and Whelehan, he speaks of Esther as 'a damaged child', provocatively expressing the view that Dickens 'is writing about a man who for some reason, can't deal with grown-up women, so what he'd like to do is groom the girl' and comments that 'he didn't have to make it so easy on [John] Jarndyce'.[111] In later interviews, this softens somewhat so that the reference to abuse and grooming is dropped while the idea of the 'severely damaged child' who 'starts the story with a pretty low self-image' is retained.[112] At the de Montfort session in February 2005, Davies acknowledges that Esther's ignorance of her origins has been problematic for her but reworks it, rather clumsily, into a common problem for modern children:

> she also starts from a position that, in fact, more and more kids start from today, in that she doesn't know who her parents are exactly and she is kind of looking for a mum in a hopeless kind of way, never expecting to find her.[113]

4. The awkwardness of Esther and Jarndyce

Davies does not however use the notion of the damaged child to offer insights into the things he dislikes about Esther. Instead his solution is to emphasise that Esther is 'useful, intelligent, practical': 'I worked on ... her sharp insights, her refusal to be taken in ... her quickness to see practical solutions'.[114] Leavis had compared Esther to Jane Austen's most difficult-to-like heroine, Fanny Price, in *Mansfield Park* (1814) and, while Davies does not quite make his difficult-to-like Esther into a modern Elizabeth Bennet, in 'spic[ing] up her empathetic and loving nature with a bit of spikiness', he does seek to imbue her with the same kind of spirit that had marked the heroine of his 1995 *Pride and Prejudice*.[115] This greater resilience in Esther allows for a further softening towards Jarndyce (Denis Lawson). Davies tells Giddings that 'Jarndyce's realisation that he has made a mistake and that he must relinquish Esther, is perhaps the most poignant moment in the story'. On the DVD commentary for the final episode, he expresses sympathy for Jarndyce, who has to reject what he most wants – sex with Esther – and Stafford-Clark comments wryly that 'Andrew and I feel for Jarndyce' (fig. 4).

Much of the publicity connecting *Bleak House* to soap opera focused on serialisation and thus avoided references to other features of soap opera; such an approach suggests a residual belief that the classic serial was qualitatively different from a soap opera and that a more detailed comparison of subject matter could have been problematic. But the problem of Esther indicates something rather different. Esther Summerson is indeed a challenging character inspiring a long history of critical disagreement. Her story and the way it has been told has led to feminist readings of her character, seeking to explain and reclaim those characteristics which make her so unpopular. In these accounts, Esther's troublesome characteristics are as strongly associated with her past as the more practical and clear-headed qualities which Davies brings to the fore in his solution to the problem. In doing so, he played down the feminine orientation of the narration, the melodramatic engagement with the public world through an expression of feeling and the possibility of understanding the story from a female viewpoint. In other words, Davies and the writing team eschewed the common approach of soaps which is to take stories of sexuality and abuse and present them, with the force of melodrama, through the victim's eyes.

As it happens, we can contrast Davies's retreat from the notion of Jarndyce grooming Esther, and ending up with a ruefully sympathetic account of his dilemma, with the upfront handling of a story of child abuse in the BBC's *EastEnders* in 2008/9. In this story, viewers saw an established character, fifteen-year-old Whitney (Shona McGarty) resume her sexual relationship with her adoptive mother's boyfriend, Tony King (Chris Coghill), who has been grooming her since she was twelve. As the story developed, we saw Whitney passionately declare her love for Tony and emotionally abase herself to get his attention while he, losing interest as she gets older, begins to groom one of her younger friends. The storyline took on the difficult question of the girl's dependence on and declared love for her abuser. Indeed as one of the *EastEnders*' researchers explained

> One thing that was quite difficult for me to get right was the idea [I had] that she didn't want sex. It's Whitney's way of keeping Tony happy. If she lets him do it, then he's nicer to her and he makes her feel special.[116]

The narrative showed the dawning of Whitney's reluctant understanding of Tony's betrayal, her ambivalence about giving evidence at his trial and the ongoing impact of the abuse on her subsequent sexual and familial relationships, particularly in highly emotional scenes with her mother, Bianca (Patsy Palmer). The purpose of referring to this is not to suggest that the *EastEnders* storyline was perfectly handled but to point out that the soap had a framework, in its history of handling social issues relating to women, in its melodramatic aesthetic and in its endless narrative process to take on such a story and develop it from the angle of the young woman. A spokesperson for the NSPCC praised the storyline, arguing that

> A soap opera ... allows the time and space to explore the subject in ways a 'one off' drama or documentary would never be able to. This story began in September and will continue well into next year, allowing us to portray not only the grooming and abuse but the consequences for all the individuals involved.[117]

In the long telling of this story, Whitney could certainly be as irritating as Esther. But the difference is that the full emotional impact of how she is suffering and why she behaves as she does is conveyed in a way that *Bleak House* never quite manages with Esther.

Esther is of course just one character in the story and we will explore issues of characterisation, viewpoint and narration in the following chapters. Here, I will first note that it would seem that Davies was either ignorant of the debates about Esther or chose not to refer to them to critics and/or the potential audience. I accept Davies's own view that as an adaptor he is offering 'a kind of reading of the book'[118] but I wonder whether his reading of the novel would have been richer if he had chosen to engage not only with the original source but also with something of its critical history. Second, I think the problem of Esther illustrates that, even with the apparent embrace of the popular, which this version of *Bleak House* seemed to exemplify, hierarchies of value still operate in how genres are understood and adopted. While the BBC

5. Esther's 'capacity for grief' after Woodcourt's proposal

press office and Davies were willing to embrace the serial elements of
soap opera, it would appear that the adaptor could not quite bring
himself to employ its full-blown melodramatic mode. There are
moments when Esther's capacity for grief is graphically dramatised on
screen (fig. 5), particularly in the final episode after Woodcourt's
proposal but Esther never finds the words to express what she feels. An
adaptation can trigger thoughts of other possibilities and, in the back of
my mind, there flickers a wilder, more intense version of *Bleak House*
in which Esther finally finds the voice to speak back to those who
abandoned her ...

41

4 Narrative Organisation and the Double Story

One expectation of adaptations generally is that they will retell the original plot. But this can be a difficult task. The plot of a long novel is complex and different readers will see different events as particularly important or crucial. Previous adaptations may have popularised their own narrative organisation of the original as was the case with David Lean's versions of *Great Expectations* (1946) and *Oliver Twist* (1948). And too much plot in too short a time will render the adaptation hard to follow and leave little space to flesh out characterisation or theme. Despite the fact that many critics agree that *Bleak House* is Dickens's best-constructed novel, Davies characteristically argued that 'when you get down to it the plot doesn't quite work'.[119] In this section, I want to look at how *Bleak House* (2005) organised its complex narrative across fifteen episodes, bearing in mind some of the arguments about serialisation and suspense discussed earlier.

Narrative organisation is both complex and interesting in *Bleak House* (2005) because it deploys two different kinds of narrative structure, two different ways of telling a story. The adaptation does not adopt the dual narration of the novel, in which the story is told partly by Esther and partly by a third-person narrator. It is hardly surprising that the TV version does not use Esther as narrator, given Davies's attitude to her and the current disapproval of voiceovers in screenwriting practices. Nevertheless, there is a clear division in the adaptation which is based not so much on the content of the story (the Chancery story, the Dedlock story) but on the mode of storytelling. The first is what we might call a forward-looking, open mode of narration in which the conclusion is in the unwritten future and characters gradually work towards it through a series of events which make that future possible and, in the end, inevitable. This is the mode of the romance in which two (mismatched) people meet, work out their initial hostilities and in the end resolve to live their future lives together. It is also the mode of the *bildungsroman* or coming-of-age novel, in which the principal character is educated, leaves home and learns what the world is like and how to live in it; it is comparable to what modern screenwriting parlance calls the story of a 'journey'. The second mode is the deductive mode, in which the initial event (often a mysterious death) occurs before the story starts and has become enigmatic or obscured by the time the narration begins. The conclusion, which involves the reconstitution of this event so that its meaning can be clearly seen, is thus set in the past and the narrative involves piecing possible elements together into different patterns which are tested against the established facts until the final and true version is found. This is the mode of the detective story, the mystery tale, the police procedural and the film noir and the denouement involves the identification of those who have been guilty of past crimes and betrayals. Todorov distinguished between these two types of narrative logic by suggesting that

> One unfolds on a horizontal line: we want to know what each event provokes, what it *does*. The other represents a series of variations which stack up along a vertical line: what we look for in each event is what it *is*. The first is a narrative of contiguity, the second a narrative of substitutions.[120]

These contrasting types of structural organisation are useful for the purpose of analysis and are not intended as a set of mutually exclusive rules. Soap operas offer a clear example of the forward-looking mode, in which events and actions propel characters forward to an unknown

43

future but their use of particular stories of long-lost relatives or past misdeeds can fall into the deductive mode. *Bleak House* (2005) is striking for the way in which it engages these two modes of storytelling and strongly associates them with different characters.

The forward-looking narrative of contiguity in the serial combines the romance narrative with the coming-of-age story, threading it through the stories of Richard (Patrick Kennedy), Ada (Carey Mulligan) and Esther, the three young people whose lives are brought together in the first episode. Although only Richard and Ada are wards of court, the narrative presents all three as unformed young characters who are looking forward to the next stage of their lives and who are indeed required to develop (differently gendered) prospects. Viewers might expect their stories to be optimistic and for their endings to involve romantic liaison and social success but the fact that the three first meet in front of the Lord High Chancellor, in the Court of Chancery, who agrees that they can go and live at Bleak House with Jarndyce as their guardian, might give pause for thought. Part of their task will be to take control of their own lives, with all three finding this difficult. But each of these young characters does change and, while initially bound together through friendship as well as circumstances, the narrative shows that their individual actions generate serious consequences for all.

Richard is thus set up as a handsome, confident, carefree young man aware that he needs to get out into the world. He literally tests out his prospects with his brief apprenticeships in medicine and the law and a longer period in the army which concludes in episode 11. But he gradually becomes absorbed with the Jarndyce case, a danger specifically warned against by his guardian. In the final four episodes, this has become his sole preoccupation and his future is thus fatally bound up with the outcome of the case; he collapses in Chancery when the case is declared void because the costs have eaten up the value of the disputed estate. Richard's storyline demonstrates that lack of movement in a story can actually be a narrative event. In episode 10, one scene shows Richard protesting to his lawyer, Vholes (Dermot Crowley), that

6. Richard leaves Vholes's office and disappears into the streets

nothing is happening in the case. It finishes with a high shot, from Vholes's viewpoint, of Richard in his military uniform leaving the office and moving up the street; the contrast between the bright red splash of his jacket and the slump of his shoulders indicates that Richard's downward slide has progressed another notch (fig. 6). As Dickens put it in his mems on Chapter XXXIX: 'Richard's decline – <u>Carry on</u>'.[121] On his deathbed, in the final episode, Richard demonstrates that he has not fully grown into an understanding of the world which has failed him: 'Everything's come clear', he says to Ada, 'we can start the world all over again.' But he does apologise to both Ada and Jarndyce for the wrongs he has done them and in that sense achieves the self-knowledge typical of this narrative mode.

Ada's story is also developed through this forward-looking mode of narration though her gender lends it a different inflection. In fact, Richard's ventures into the world take him out of the story for quite long periods whereas Ada's love for Esther and her residence with Jarndyce up until episode 13 mean that she remains a central figure even though very little actually happens to her. The relationship between her and Richard is heavily prefigured in episode 1, is settled between them by episode 3 and never wavers thereafter meaning that there is no

45

element of suspense in this romance. Instead, the development of her character is marked by her declarations of independence from the judgments being made about Richard and herself by Jarndyce and Esther. These declarations, which give her some of the flavour of the independent heroine of costume drama discussed in the previous chapter, are provoked not just by her love for Richard but by the hurtful discovery that secrets are being kept from her. While Richard's narrative trajectory is marked by the testing out of unsuccessful situations, Ada's is marked by repetitions which remind the audience of her consistency. Thus in episode 9 she is gently worried that Esther is keeping some trouble from her; in episode 11 she twice protests at Jarndyce's attitude to Richard; and in episode 13 she announces to Esther her intention to live with Richard since they have been secretly married. Ada thus establishes some kind of autonomy through rebelling against the attitudes of both her friend and her guardian. But Ada comes to further knowledge which Richard cannot. With her pregnancy she begins to reach an adult understanding of her world, fearing that even the birth of the child will not precipitate any change in Richard; at last, she expresses sorrow and doubt about Richard's actions (fig. 7). With his death, the birth of their child takes her into an unknown future beyond the end of the book.

Esther's story shares some of this sense of change and growth. Unlike Ada and Richard, she enters Bleak House with a job as companion and housekeeper (fig. 8) and more generally as someone who cares for and helps others. This is a role which she is seen to enjoy and be good at, running Bleak House effectively and seeking to help those in need like Charley (Katie Angelou), Jo (Harry Eden)and Caddy (Natalie Press). Unlike Ada therefore, Esther's future is not dependent on a romantic relationship and, after her illness, she declares to Jarndyce that 'I should not think there is a man in the world who'd want to marry a pockmarked nobody like me.' Nevertheless, the audience knows that this is untrue and her heroine's status, within a classic serial, has led us to expect that her most important narrative act will be a choice of husband. She indeed receives proposals from three men: the legal clerk,

7. Ada speaks of her fears for Richard

8. Esther at work at Bleak House

Mr Guppy (Burn Gorman); her guardian, John Jarndyce; and the self-effacing, good doctor, Allan Woodcourt (Richard Harrington) (figs 9, 10 and 11).

As with Ada and Richard, there are signs as the serial develops that Esther is growing into an independent person. She learns how to deal with busybodies and hangers-on such as Mrs Woodcourt (Di

9. Esther's suitors: Guppy unsuccessfully woos Esther ...

10. Jarndyce awkwardly falls in love with Esther ...

11. Woodcourt unsuccessfully proposes to Esther

Botcher) and Mr Skimpole (Nathaniel Parker); she comes to terms with the disfiguring scars left by her illness; and she is stronger in taking action in, for instance, helping to get Sergeant George (Hugo Speer) out of jail. But, unlike Ada, Esther does not learn enough to make herself independent and she continues to feel that she is unlovable. Her capacity to grow and make her own choices is blocked; although she turns Guppy down twice, faced with the choice between Woodcourt and Jarndyce, she can only declare to the former 'I am not free to love you' and tell the latter 'I love you' even as he tells her that they cannot marry. In the end, the choice is taken out of her hands.

What blocks the full development of the coming-of-age narrative for Esther is her involvement in the other narrative mode – the narrative of deduction. But before turning to this, I want to make a further point about the narrative of contiguity which I have been applying to these three central characters. The openness of this mode of storytelling means that it can encompass a host of other characters and stories without breaking the narrative thread. As they move on, the central characters brush up against other characters with their own stories which can be explored even though they have relatively little impact on the main story. Dickens uses this mode extensively to accommodate the huge range of characters in his novels and those adapting his works have to decide how much room they have for these stories branching off the main trunk. Thus in *Bleak House* (2005), we get the story of Caddy Jellaby and her marriage into the Turveydrop family; the story of Mr Skimpole, the apparently guileless sponger who proves to be amoral and dangerous; the stories of Mr Gridley (Tony Haygarth) and Miss Flite caught up in Chancery; that of Mr Boythorn (Warren Clarke) who, despite his fierce feud with Sir Leicester Dedlock (Timothy West), is unstintingly kind to his friends; and of the orphan Charley who becomes Esther's maid. The openness of this structure also allows for similar stories with a different emphasis to develop at the same time, so that, for instance, the engagement of Caddy parallels the love affair of Richard and Ada; for events to be foreshadowed as the death of Gridley foreshadows that of Richard; and for characters to

49

leave and return in a rather different position as Woodcourt does after his time at sea. For Dickens's enthusiasts, eight hours is not enough for the full range of stories in the novel but nevertheless the adaptation does give some autonomy to these stories while, as the novel does, also weaving them into the overall narrative.

This narrative mode of deduction in *Bleak House* (2005) serves to tell a different kind of story from that of the three young people: the story of Esther's birth and the downfall of her father, Hawdon (known as Nemo) (John Lynch), and her mother, Lady Dedlock (Gillian Anderson). The content of this story has the traditional elements of melodrama – the fallen woman, the illegitimate child, the family secrets and pressures to conform to social expectations – which were familiar to Dickens and his readers through their dramatisation in popular theatre. In 1961, literary critic A. O. J. Cockshut could write that the Dedlock story was 'a part of the novel which no one, I suppose, regards as wholly satisfactory' because of its association with this strain of melodrama.[122] That would not be the critical view today and the makers of *Bleak House* certainly relished this story. Stafford-Clark found it to be 'probably the single main narrative strand in terms of driving the thing forward' while Davies commented of the scenes between Lady Dedlock and Tulkinghorn (Charles Dance), the lawyer who pursues her, that 'in contemporary terms [i.e. at the time of the adaptation] these are the best written scenes in the book'.[123]

It is worth noting that for Dickens's contemporaries the melodramatic content would have been more familiar than the deductive mode of the telling. Inspector Bucket (Alun Armstrong), who finally resolves this part of the story, was the first police detective in the English novel and stems from Dickens's consistent interest in the police and law enforcement. For modern audiences, however, detective work carried out by police, private eyes or others has become a familiar and central feature of television drama. This adaptation retains some of the melodrama of the story, particularly in its positioning of both Esther and her mother as victims afforded no opportunity to challenge those who harm them. As we shall see, though, a compelling *serialised* narrative is delivered by framing this melodrama within the deductive narrative mode, so that the piecing together of the secrets in Esther's past is seen to be achieved through the activities of a variety of detectives.

The advantage of the deductive mode is that it sets up a suspenseful relationship between the investigator and those being investigated, with the initial event posited as emblematic of a threat to order. The compulsion to solve the original mystery assumes a social significance, with the discovery of the truth becoming a way of assigning guilt for what is wrong in society. But the nature of the mystery, the object of investigation and the characters undertaking the detective work can all change as the story progresses, which is important in giving impetus to a long serial like *Bleak House*. Thus, the first mystery, signalled in episode 1, is the question of Esther's origins and that remains a key element not explicated until her meeting with Lady Dedlock in episode 8 nor resolved until Lady Dedlock's death in episode 14. But this initial mystery is bolstered by a number of other events and enigmas which have to be resolved including the identity of Nemo; the identity of 'the lady' who seeks from Jo, the homeless roadsweeper, a tour of all the places associated with Nemo; the murder of the Dedlocks' family lawyer, Tulkinghorn; and the whereabouts of Lady Dedlock once she has finally fled from the revelation of her past. So, while the puzzle of Esther's identity and Lady Dedlock's transgression remains central, the answer is pieced together through solving a number of other mysteries along the way.

The object of investigation remains stable, however, in *Bleak House* (2005): Lady Dedlock. This lends the pursuit for truth a relentlessness with Lady Dedlock the focus of the suspicion and questioning. Even when others are also the subject of suspicion, as when George is arrested for Tulkinghorn's murder, Lady Dedlock continues to be questioned and her bedroom searched. While Lady Dedlock is a constant as the main object of investigation, a range of investigators is set against her, since this side of the story is 'full of unsuccessful detectives'.[124] At first it seems as if Esther might investigate her own past as the audience becomes privy to information about her childhood

12. Esther seeks knowledge of her mother

13. 'Your mother, Esther, is your disgrace and you hers' says Miss Barbary

through flashbacks showing her memories (figs 12 and 13), which occur on the coach journey taking her to her new life at Bleak House. But she is quickly replaced by others so that the story then proceeds through the work of three main detectives. Guppy begins to dig around in the first episode, driven by an interest in Esther as a possible marriage prospect, and works away at a possible connection between her and Lady

Dedlock which might be mutually beneficial. He is still active in episode 14 when he revisits Lady Dedlock. Tulkinghorn is the most implacable of the investigators. Alerted to a possible scandal by Lady Dedlock's extreme reaction to the sight of (Nemo's) handwriting on legal documents, his investigations into her past throw out such a wide net that they pull various other characters such as Krook (Johnny Vegas), Smallweed (Phil Davis) and George into the story. Tulkinghorn continually tests out explanatory stories based on the latest information her has elicited, most strikingly in episode 9, when he demonstrates his power over Lady Dedlock by relating his version of her relationship with Nemo, without naming the parties, to the ignorant Sir Leicester and his fearful, guilt-ridden wife. The four scenes in which Tulkinghorn questions Lady Dedlock provide not just the central thread of the deductive story but its most powerful image of the two confronting each other and attempting to gauge each other's knowledge in coded conversation. Or as Dickens put it in his mems: 'Mr Tulkinghorn and Lady Dedlock. Each watching the other. Open that interest and leave them so –'.[125] (figs 35 and 36) The third of the main investigators, Inspector Bucket, is brought in by Tulkinghorn in episode 4, specifically to find out what Jo knows about Nemo and 'the lady'. Bucket takes over completely after Tulkinghorn's death, correctly identifying his murderer as Hortense (Lilo Baur), Lady Dedlock's French maid, but failing to find Lady Dedlock in time to make her aware of Sir Leicester's forgiveness.

But these three detective figures are joined by various freelance investigators who hope to gain something from their scraps of knowledge. Krook, for instance, the collector of paper in his rag-and-bottle shop, holds but cannot read the letters written by Lady Dedlock ('smells of ladies, love letters') to her ex-lover, now lodging under Krook's own roof. Smallweed takes over the shop after Krook's death and seeks to profit by using the letters for blackmail; after first selling them to Tulkinghorn, Smallweed finally uses them to inform Sir Leicester of his wife's guilt. Jo is the opposite of these characters hunting for knowledge with sinister intent since he has knowledge which either no-one listens to, as at Nemo's inquest, or which it troubles him to exploit. But even his inadequate knowledge contributes to the picture; both his denial that Hortense was 'the lady' who asked to be shown the places connected with Nemo and his confused identification of Esther as 'the lady', i.e. as her own mother, helps to move the plot along.

Having established these overarching modes of narration, we turn next to look at how they work in terms of the episodic serial structure. Chapter 3 examined how the production team viewed serialisation as one important way to fulfil the object of keeping the audience in suspense. Speed of action and suspense were key factors. The DVD commentary for episode 1 observes that scenes needed to be short and Davies relates this to soap-opera practices.[126] The scenes are frequently much shorter than those in an average *EastEnders* episode, with the result that the episode as a whole moves at a faster pace and could be compared more readily to the British soap aimed at teenagers, *Hollyoaks* (1995–). Another example of this emphasis on speed is the handling of the opening of each episode. *Bleak House* follows the convention of beginning each episode with one or more establishing shots, allowing the viewer to identify where the scene is taking place. But, after the credits, the episode opens with two or three speedily edited shots, accompanied by music or electronic sound, a pattern quickly established as the way of indicating location throughout the serial. The viewer is thus given narrative information but with an abrupt jolt rather than the conventionally smooth transition. The impact of this is even more striking when the initial shot is not a static view of a conventional landscape or house but a close-up or a zoom shot on movement (figs 14 and 15). In the case of the latter, this device serves to create the effects of drama and speed, underlined by the fact that this striking opening to the last episode is followed by a sombre and reflective scene in which Sir Leicester visits his dead wife's tomb.

The production team sought to create suspense as well as maintain a rapid action pace and stressed the importance of cliff-hangers as a means of ensuring that the audience would want to return. Episodes endings were thus crucial and, by looking at the final shots of each episode, we can see how the need to introduce and maintain

54

14. The beginning of episode 13

15. The beginning of episode 15

suspense had the effect of throwing weight on to the detective element, since twelve out of the fifteen episodes end with an image from the deductive narrative. (See Appendix A). Only three episodes end with an image from the *bildungsroman* narrative and two of these occur early in the series, offering a reflective moment rather than a cliff-hanger: in episode 3, Esther smiles at the gift of Woodcourt's posy and in episode 5 the scene showing Gridley's death finishes with a close-up of a thoughtful Richard. (The third such image which finishes episode 15 and the serial as a whole will be discussed below.) It is worth questioning whether the need for suspense rendered this reliance on the deductive narrative inevitable. There certainly were possibilities in the other side of the story; for instance, when Jarndyce proposes to Esther, she asks for time to consider but the proposal and waiting period are managed entirely within episode 10, so that Esther's decision is not left to hang between episodes.

The use of images from the deductive narrative at the end of episodes can be examined further. It is worth noting the high proportion of real cliff-hangers in this group – that is to say endings which are returned to at the beginning of the next episode. Such cliff-hangers, as I have indicated in Chapter 3, are actually not particularly common in *EastEnders* but in *Bleak House* we have six of them at the end of episodes 1, 4, 6, 11, 12 and 13. Sometimes, these cliff-hangers feel rather forced as, for instance, when Jo's identification of Hortense as the lady at the end of episode 4 is immediately withdrawn by him at the beginning of episode 5. Nevertheless, they show clearly how the investigative narrative yields mechanisms to promote suspense across episodes. The close-up of George at the end of episode 10 is one of a number of pointers putting him in the frame for Tulkinghorn's murder, while a close-up of an anonymous note identifying Lady Dedlock as the murderer closes episode 12 and a close-up of Hortense at the end of episode 13 reinforces the surprise of Bucket's order to arrest her for the murder rather than Lady Dedlock.

The dominant face at episode endings is that of Tulkinghorn, with four episodes finishing with close-ups of his thoughtful face and brooding eyes (and there is a fifth such close-up in the middle of the hour-long first episode). The last such close-up is of his face after he has been killed but the other images illustrate his response to a specific narrative event – the death of Nemo (episode 1, fig. 16), Jo's misidentification of 'the lady' (episode 4) and Lady Dedlock's visit to his room (episode 9, fig. 17). This tendency to feature Tulkinghorn in a

16. Tulkinghorn discovers the dead Nemo at the end of episode 1

17. Tulkinghorn watches Lady Dedlock at the end of episode 9

reflective shot at an episode end underlines the dominance of his role as the ruthless investigator who drives the story forward. By contrast, Esther takes the final shot in the deductive narrative three times and five times in all, though not always with a close-up and on two occasions with other people. This is an indication that she plays an important part in the Dedlock story but the range of different moods and postures indicates that her role is flexible and that she moves across both narrative modes. This balancing of Esther and Tulkinghorn in the cliff-hanger position points to another (hidden) element of the narrative organisation; while Tulkinghorn focuses so rigidly on Lady Dedlock, he cannot see that Esther is part of the story.

While noting the suspense generated by the episode endings, it is also important to recognise that the narrative does at times allow for pause and reflection. Sometimes this is equated with major set pieces, with a large number of characters assembled together; the death of Jo, for instance, brings together more characters than the same scene in the book, the pace of the filming slows and the visual effects are subdued. Other moments are less significant in narrative terms but work visually to reinforce a narrative point and are marked by picturesque compositions which are carefully framed and held. Thus, Richard's conversation with Skimpole in episode 2, about the (false) possibilities of the Jarndyce case, is presented by alternating side-on tracking shots of them companionably walking together in the garden with a repeated long shot in which they gradually approach the viewer but are ominously framed by foliage and the dark tracery of the iron gate ahead of them. In episode 9, a long shot held from above of Richard and Ada,

18. A striking composition is a reminder of Richard and Ada's love

embracing on the grass (fig. 18), acts as a visual reminder of their youth and passion before a cut to a close-up takes up their story again.

The two narrative modes provide two different but interrelated endings to the serial as a whole. The deductive mode effectively finishes in episode 14. At the beginning of the episode, Bucket successfully identifies Hortense as Tulkinghorn's killer and the episode ends with the death of Lady Dedlock, finally chased down by Bucket to the gate of the graveyard where Hawdon is buried. The mystery is solved and some kind of emotional resolution is reached. Esther, in a strict narrative sense, has teamed with Bucket to hound her own mother to death but evidence that Lady Dedlock colludes with the exposure of her own guilt is to be found in her letter to Esther, begging for forgiveness, the letter which gives Bucket a clue to her whereabouts. In the final scene of the episode, Esther holds her mother protectively and a flicker of recognition in Lady Dedlock's eyes indicates reconciliation. David Miller (1983) suggests that the deductive mode involves a continual refining away of narrative material so that only the key facts which will finally reveal the truth remain to resolve the narrative. Episode 14 is representative of this distillation. With Hawdon in his nearby grave, the three members of the original, natural and fatal family are at last brought together. The mystery is explained but, although order is restored, the damage caused by the original trauma is beyond remedy. This is another moment when the visual composition enforces a narrative pause. The embrace of Esther and her mother reminds us of the previous meeting, when Lady Dedlock made her revelations in the Ghost Walk, and they appear as one body with only Esther's head visible; the framing of the image, as the shadow of the graveyard's railings fall across them and the fabric of their skirts sweeps in the mud, imbues this moment with a visual richness to mark the Deadlock story (figs 19 and 20).

This leaves the final thirty-minute episode to resolve the issues raised in the other narrative mode, of which there are plenty; Davies remarked on the DVD commentary for episode 15 that 'it was nice to have this much story left' so that they were 'not just tying up loose ends'.

59

19. The dying Lady Dedlock looks at her daughter

20. Esther holds her mother at the end of episode 14

This episode covers the final outcome of the *Jarndyce* v *Jarndyce* case with the brief flare of hope for Richard and Ada when the new will is found, followed by the crushing news that the case had exhausted itself through its own costs; the death of Richard; and Jarndyce's final gift of Esther to Allan Woodcourt along with a second Bleak House in which they can live a happy future life. The difficulties of adapting Dickens's much criticised happy ending can be seen in the 1985 *Bleak House*, which ends with the birth of Ada and Richard's child. Ada, watched by Woodcourt who has presumably assisted at the birth, passes the new baby, Richard, to Esther, who hands the child to the nervous Jarndyce. Jarndyce and Esther smile at each other, while posed together with the child between them while Esther repeats to Jarndyce Richard's final exhortation to 'Begin the World.' This bringing together of Jarndyce and Esther as if they were the couple looking forward to the future (fig. 21) exposes some of the problems of the novel's ending and confirms the rather muted tone of this adaptation. The 2005 *Bleak House* takes a rather different approach, embracing the pastoral idyll provided by Dickens. It ends with a prolonged scene celebrating the marriage of Esther and Woodcourt which embraces the way that the narrative of contiguity does not so much select key facts to explain the past as allow for as many narrative elements as possible to be bundled together in anticipating the future. So in this mode of narration, the final scene, rather than focusing on Esther's original, past family, celebrates the family created by the serial. The final dance features not only those whom Esther treats as a substitute family – Ada, Jarndyce, Boythorn, Charley and the Turveydrops – but also those who have contributed to the developing stories of the three young people, even the reprehensible

61

21. Final shots: Esther and Jarndyce hold young Richard (*Bleak House*, 1985)

22. Esther and Woodcourt kiss at the end of *Bleak House* (2005)

Skimpole. Some of the characters have had a foot in the other story, in particular George, Phil (Michael Smiley) and Mrs Rouncewell (Anne Reid) but only Inspector Bucket represents the detectives; Krook, Tulkinghorn, Smallweed and even Guppy have been expunged. This ending celebrates the restoration of the proper, patriarchal order, with Jarndyce literally giving Esther to Woodcourt but the swooping and encircling camera also celebrates a heterogeneous version of the family in which all sorts of characters can find a place. This ending heralds the future, symbolised by Ada and Richard's baby as well as the happiness of the couple whose long kiss provides the final image (fig. 22).[127] In some ways, this has similarities with the final episode of the British soap *Brookside* in 2003 when cast and crew gathered in the close to bid farewell to the faithful audience. But rather interestingly, it actually presents a more emphatic ending than the book, in which the reader is left hanging, as if in a soap opera, as Esther fails to complete the sentence she is writing, leaving the book to finish with the words 'even supposing ...'.

5 Characterisation and Performance

As we saw in Chapter 3, the production team for *Bleak House* looked to the suspense generated by serialisation as the chief method of maintaining audience interest. But the fact that they were adapting a Dickens novel and drawing on soap opera as a format also suggests the importance of characterisation. Dickens's novels are known as much for their characters as for their stories and actors performing them often have a strong sense of the physicality and robustness of a Dickens character. Miriam Margoyles for instance talks about his characters as having 'such defined shapes' while Martin Jarvis refers to Dickens's descriptions as stage directions which conjure up the character, citing the depiction of Uriah Heep's facial expression as dictating to the actor how the character will speak: 'You've only got to look into the text to really glean all you need in order to inhabit truthfully what Dickens was after'.[128] Similarly, soap-opera producers and writers will talk about the importance of characters, stressing that the stories soaps tell and the issues they take up have to fit the established characters rather than the other way round. In addition, Dickens's novels and television soap operas both work with very large casts of characters; the organisation of such casts is a challenge, not just in terms of production logistics, as Stafford-Clark asserted, but also in terms of giving them enough scope to generate narrative understanding and emotional feeling in the audience.

I have argued in relation to the British soap *Coronation Street* that soap characters are managed and understood both in terms of how they conform to certain narrative functions and serial types and by the characteristics allotted to them which allow us to identify them as individuals.[129] The same mode of analysis works well with *Bleak House* (2005). I will also consider the question of how far characters can be understood through their external attributes and to what extent we are privy to their internal motivations and thoughts. This is sometimes seen as a fundamental distinction between films and novels, a difference based on a perceived contrast between the realist attention to surface detail furnished by the camera and the novel's use of words to get inside someone's head. Dickens provides an interesting case, since his characters often derived believability from the highly unrealistic exaggeration and repetition of some key physical attribute or phrase which has the cumulative effect of lending the character a quality of intense, if narrow, life.[130]

In a screen adaptation, of course, the characters are also given life through the way in which they are performed. The audience is expected to understand the meaning of a physical gesture or a look and acting is used to convey the characters' inner feelings. Acting is indeed one of the pleasures offered to the audience by the classic serial and is highlighted in the overt difference between actor and character. Whereas, in soaps, actors often seem to become the characters they play over the years, in classic serials, acting is noticed and valued; the actors may be doing something different from their previous roles while imbuing their parts with connotations derived from their images as celebrities or stars.

The publicity for *Bleak House* emphasised the importance of casting, stressing in particular the number of actors who had been keen to take part. The press pack applauds Dickens and the BBC for the creation and casting of over forty principal roles: 'Charles Dickens created a cornucopia of characters in *Bleak House* and the new BBC version complements that with the range and breadth of talent playing them', it states, quoting Stafford-Clark on the importance of securing 'known faces from a variety of different backgrounds, all known to the audience that we are trying to attract'. We can see in the casting the range of different audiences which the serial is trying to capture. Gillian Anderson, from *The X Files* (1993–2002) but with experience of period drama in *The House of Mirth* (2000), was in Stafford-Clark's words 'a big star … a household name'. She followed Diana Rigg in *Bleak House* (1985) in bringing glamour to the production which is justified more by the need to carry a starring role than by reference to the book. Charles Dance had a different kind of following with a long screen career specialising in adaptations and period drama, from *The Jewel in the Crown* (1984) to *Gosford Park* (2001), while Timothy West and Richard Griffiths were perhaps more strongly associated with theatre. Dance's previous roles as a romantic hero would also lend his Tulkinghorn an interesting allure, not available to Peter Vaughn in the 1985 version. In other parts, we can see actors who, while not necessarily being immediately identifiable by name, would be familiar for their work in television dramas, such as Alun Armstrong, Pauline Collins, Phil Davis, Anne Reid and Ian Richardson; comedians like Catherine Tate, Alistair McGowan and Johnny Vegas; well-known actors in small cameo roles like Sheila Hancock and Liza Tarbuck; and familiar faces from soaps, Charlie Brooks and Roberta Taylor from *EastEnders* and Dennis Lawson from *Holby City* (1999–). Despite Stafford-Clark's emphasis on known faces, *Bleak House* followed a familiar strategy for a classic serial in casting relative unknowns in the young parts, though these did have some experience: Anna Maxwell Martin had appeared in the BBC's classic serial, *North and South*, in the previous year; Carey Mulligan was cast before her appearance as Kitty Bennet in *Pride and Prejudice* (2005) had been seen in cinemas; and Patrick Kennedy had some BBC television experience. The size of the cast and the range of styles and experience made the press office's claim that 'their skills have blended seamlessly to recreate Dickensian England' a bold one.

We have seen that *Bleak House* (2005) featured a number of characters in the role of detectives, able to advance the mystery plot while adopting different modes of investigation. The same kind of grouping around narrative function can be seen with other characters and helps both to suggest the themes of the serial and identify characters with particular kinds of narrative activity or position. The groups include:

1   the neglected or orphaned children – Esther, Jo, Charley and her siblings, Caddy, Rosa, Ada and Richard;
2   the neglectful or self-obsessed parents – Mrs Jellaby, Skimpole, Mr Turveydrop (Matthew Kelly), Mrs Guppy, Mrs Woodcourt, Lady Dedlock;
3   the thwarted fathers or men who should have married – Jarndyce, Boythorn, George;
4   the witnesses to some aspect of the mystery – Nemo, Jo, Jenny (Charlie Brooks), Lady Dedlock, Jarndyce, Esther, Aunt Barbary (Kelly Hunter), Hortense;
5   Esther's helpers –Jarndyce, Guppy, Boythorn, Woodcourt, Miss Flite, Jenny, George, Mrs Rouncewell, Snagsby (Sean McGinley), Jo, Bucket;
6   the hinderers – Skimpole, Snagsby, Vholes, Lady Dedlock, Hortense;
7   the detectives – Esther, Tulkinghorn, Bucket, Krook, Smallweed, Guppy;
8   Esther's suitors – Guppy, Jarndyce, Woodcourt.

These groupings are relatively flexible and a character can belong to more than one. This is partly due to the double narrative but fulfilling more than one function can indicate a more complex character or at least one with different aspects. This is clearly the case with major characters such as Esther but it can also govern how less dominant characters are understood. In the first episode, for instance, Guppy is positioned as a helper to Esther on her arrival in London, but the subsequent overlap between his activity as a suitor and a detective (he both spies on and for Esther) invests his character with an ambiguous edge. Contrast that with the characterisation of Woodcourt, whose combined role of suitor and helper makes him ubiquitous but monotonously good.

These largely narrative or thematic groupings can be set alongside groupings based on other social factors. Particularly important in the classic serial is the element of class. Woodcourt is a doctor, a profession which for modern audiences reinforces his virtuous character and his suitability as a suitor while Guppy's lowly role as legal clerk tends to undermine his courtship of Esther once she is established in the home of the wealthy Jarndyce. The interaction of narrative position and class status works differently in different cases and can be used effectively to distinguish between minor characters who might otherwise seem rather similar. Thus, Rosa and Charley both hold the class position of lady's maids and thus their fates are to be determined by others; Rosa (Emma Williams) is 'adopted' first by Mrs Rouncewell and then, more ambiguously, by Lady Dedlock while Charley is Jarndyce's 'present' to Esther. But they are distinguished by their different positions as abandoned children. Charley's character is established in her first scene, in which she demonstrates how, despite the death of her father, she is determined to keep her small family out of the orphanage (fig. 23). Rosa's past, on the other hand, is less clear; Hortense describes her as the daughter of a 'pig man' who has attracted the son of the wealthy factory owner. This affords her something of a fairytale quality and she moves

67

23. 'We're all right' Charley tells her helpers

24. Rosa leaves discussion of her future to others

through the story at the behest of others with an air of dreamy half-engagement (fig. 24). In these rather different traits, both Charley and Rosa relate to more complex aspects of Esther's character.

On top of this, particular traits and motivations can be attached to key characters, encouraging the audience to recognise their individuality. Guppy, for instance, as well as carrying various narrative functions and occupying a clear social position, is individuated through comedy. This runs right through from the first episode, when he is horrified at the prospect of appearing in Chancery with an ink-stained nose to the last, when his final unsuccessful proposal to Esther ends in humiliation thanks to his overbearing mother. The physical comedy which supports this individualisation can be seen in the precise gestures with which Burn Gorman flicks back the tails of his coat as he sits down, sniffs when the Jellaby front door slams in his face and glides out of the room while making his final exit. Guppy is an example of a character who has to be created out of his external characteristics and Gorman's performance was widely praised, not just for its humour, but for its capacity to engender sympathy for the character's feelings.

Dickens's characters are noted for their remarkable consistency. Their creation depends on the 'reiteration ... of an identity which remains exactly the same', the comedy often deriving from the way in which 'they blindly go on being themselves even in the presence of forces which should ... prick their bubble and annihilate them'.[131] The repeated association of a character with a particular physical attribute or mode of behaviour, often with a comic inflection, is typical of Dickens and of this adaptation. Some of the cameo roles warrant only one appearance so, for instance, the memory of Liza Tarbuck's Mrs Jellaby, neglecting her family for charitable work in Africa, has to have sufficient impact in episode 1 to stay with us as an explanation of her daughter's behaviour in later episodes. But the same narrow but intense focus can be seen in more substantial characters. Thus, we get Krook's half-affectionate, half-threatening crooning to his cat, Lady Jane (fig. 25); Smallweed's dependence on but abuse of his helpers expressed in his catchphrase 'Shake me up' (fig. 26); Mr Badger's pompous self-satisfaction combined with an oleaginous deference to his much-married wife; Snagsby's embarrassed acts of kindness; Mr Turveydrop's narcissistic concern for his own comfort; Gridley's agonised despair at his entrapment in Chancery; and Miss Flite's distracted optimism shot through with moments of clear insight. Managing this mode of characterisation can be difficult and Dickens adaptations are full of

69

25. Krook tries to read the love letters

26. Smallweed tries to 'shake up' George

roles pushed into grotesquerie by the exaggeration of key external markers, often through overacting; Sheila's Hancock's Mrs Guppy illustrates this tendency in this adaptation. But those not afforded sharply drawn individual characteristics – Woodcourt, Kenge (Alistair McGowan) perhaps, Vholes – run the risk of getting lost among such a large cast.

The interest of those defined by external markers lies in the impact of their personalities rather than their motivation or credibility as characters. But reliance on external observation does not rule out access to motivation though it requires it to be articulated or observable. The characterisation of Caddy Jellaby offers a good example of this. We meet Caddy in the first episode when she is acting as amanuensis to her distracted mother. Caddy's openness with Esther vouchsafes us direct access to her feelings about her mother's neglect of her family ('I wish I was an orphan') and her own position ('I know I'm a disgrace'). The transformation of her life when she falls in love is announced in episode 3 in a similarly straightforward manner. 'I love him so much', she tells Esther while at the same time denouncing the faults of her future father-in-law: 'he just preens about showing off his deportment'. This verbal directness is endorsed by the transformation in

27. Caddy transformed by her love for Prince Turveydrop

28. Esther delights in Caddy's joy

her blushing, animated face, which makes her look much younger once released from her mother's unloving neglect (fig. 27). This combination of forthright information about her feelings and the way her physical appearance also reflects her changing situation allows the audience access to Caddy's character in a way which appropriately associates her with notions of candour and a good heart.

This kind of direct access to feeling is used in developing other more major characters, allotting them specific scenes in which to articulate particular emotions or concerns. For much of the time, the audience is asked to read Ada's feelings through her looks and actions, her glances at Esther and Richard for instance revealing her growing love for both. But, like Caddy, Ada is a character who values clarity and this is underlined in a scene in the final episode in which the secrets thus far separating her from Esther are overcome. Compressed into one tearful scene are her anxieties about Richard's health, her hopes that their marriage might have changed him, her news about her pregnancy and her most terrible fear: 'I am afraid he won't live to see his child' (fig. 7). More complex is the case of Jarndyce. Again, the audience is generally required to deduce his feelings from his looks and actions: the glances at Esther which indicate his attraction towards her and his fidgety movements at moments of anxiety. We are also asked to understand his feelings through the things he does not do, his inability to kiss or hold Esther, for instance (figs 4 and 10). But he too is granted a scene allowing the audience to learn more directly of his hidden feelings. This occurs in episode 9 when Jarndyce is travelling with his friend Boythorn who (in his usual straightforward manner) asks whether Jarndyce means to marry Esther. Jarndyce's response – 'Is it so very ridiculous?' – is delivered with a slightly breaking voice; it indicates suppressed anger at Boythorn's laughter and offers a glimpse of Jarndyce's own uncertainty about the ambiguous position he has put himself and Esther in.

In these examples, the methods of characterisation generally work alongside the conventions of the classic adaptation. External markers such as costume, make-up and acting are used to create characters and their personalities are generated with broad strokes so as to mark strongly those who have a limited number of appearances. When needed and with major characters, in particular, we are also afforded direct access to internal motivation through dialogue. In looking at the presentation of the central heroine, however, rather different issues arise. Initially, we have the clearest example of the audience being given direct access to the internal feelings of a character when, in the first few minutes of the serial, as Esther starts her momentous journey to London, a flashback shows her, as a small child, asking the woman who has looked after her about her past: 'Will you tell me who am I exactly … . Did she [her mother] die because of me?' This yields us some knowledge about Esther's early childhood and, through the dark and distorted visual representation of faces and setting (see figs 12 and 13), some access to her feelings of fear and abandonment. The DVD commentary emphasises the narrative purpose of this flashback – 'the whole first fifty pages of back story … compressed into this one scene' – and there are suggestions that its visual strangeness is 'our way of telling the audience to keep watching. All sorts of things are going to happen that you're not expecting.' In fact, this bold way of establishing Esther's feelings about her lack of worth turns out to be misleading. The flashback is very restricted in what it shows and the device is scarcely repeated. It is visually referenced again in the first episode when Esther is trusted with the keys to Bleak House but not at other points when her sense of self wavers, such as after her face has been disfigured by smallpox. In addition, Esther's reticence and modesty mean that, although she can be quite forthright in her questions and judgments, she never gets to fully articulate her feelings.

73

Instead, the serial looks to Maxwell Martin's remarkable performance to indicate the character's emotions to the viewer and to provide 'a simulacrum for the subjective voice'.[132] Despite the emphasis on speed in the storytelling we are given the time and opportunity to understand Esther's feelings through studying her face. Whereas the more minor characters make an immediate first impression, Maxwell Martin frequently offers a grave, thoughtful but inexpressive face which takes time to respond to her experiences. Thus, it takes some seconds for her face to break into pleasure when Caddy announces her engagement (fig. 28); even longer for her to smile when she reflects in secret over Woodcourt's posy; and, during the search for Lady Dedlock, we need to watch her eyes in order to register flickers of feeling as she reads the letter sent by her mother (fig. 29). Over the fifteen episodes, Esther's

29. Esther reads her mother's letter

growing maturity and the increasing decisiveness of her moral judgments can be read through Maxwell Martin's facial expressions.

This approach to characterisation is exemplified by *Bleak House*'s frequent recourse to that staple of television – the close-up. Finding out the true feeling of a character by focusing on the face is a feature of soaps and questions about the moral meaning of an action or the validity of an emotional response are often expressed in soaps by holding onto a close-up at the end of the episode. We noted in the previous section the use of close-ups of Tulkinghorn at the end of a number of episodes but his close-ups and those of Lady Dedlock function very differently from those of Esther. For the first two, the access to the truth about a character via the face and eyes is blocked. Instead, the audience, already engaged with the unravelling of a complex mystery, is brought up against an enigmatic refusal to disclose motivation which depends as much on acting as on characterisation.

Mr Tulkinghorn offers the clearest example of this. His characterisation is partly achieved through external markers, a technique discussed earlier in relation to other characters. His fixed intensity of purpose is expressed through physical appearance and gestures. Dressed always in dark clothes, the emphasis is on the upper part of his body, the hunched shoulders, the head pushed slightly forward, the eyes prominent. Such is the intensity of his thoughtful, brooding gaze that it can carry the serial over a number of cliff-hangers (figs 16 and 17). He calculates what he is saying and speaks precisely, pronouncing the consonants with his teeth and tongue. He dominates those working for him, including the normally ebullient Smallweed, who is forced to tone down his furious remonstrances on Tulkinghorn's orders. He is extremely private, living alone and appearing to have no personal life. He rules through his access to secrets, brought to him in documents, rumours and attempted deals. Tulkinghorn provides himself with a motivation, most specifically in episode 9 when he advises Lady Dedlock that his sole consideration is Sir Leicester and the honour of the family. But it is clear that Tulkinghorn's interest is really in Lady Dedlock. His pursuit of her secret is indeed melodramatic, going well beyond overt reason and hinting at something within Tulkinghorn that can only find expression in the achievement of emotional power. There is a history of critical interest in Tulkinghorn who is described by various critics as the 'presiding genius' of the novel; a misogynist who hates Lady Dedlock and 'all women for their role in life and that irrational nature which he can't control'; and the holder of confidences and secrets who blocks the connections that make for true relationships.[133] In this adaptation, the gap between his proclaimed motivation and the profound damage he inflicts on himself and his victim is filled by Charles Dance's acting, which renders Tulkinghorn both powerful and enigmatic.

Dance's Tulkinghorn is balanced by Gillian Anderson as Lady Dedlock; the two share four long scenes in which he probes for her weaknesses and she both seeks information she needs and tests out her own capacity to resist his claims over her. Lady Dedlock is a more complex character than Tulkinghorn and we are granted greater access to her inner life. This is particularly the case in the episode 8 scene in which she finally meets her daughter and tries to offer some account of what has happened. She explains that after her child's supposed death she thought 'I would never feel again, nor did I until now', describes her decision to marry Sir Leicester as 'wicked' and offers family honour (the same reason as Tulkinghorn) as her explanation for refusing to see Esther again. In doing so, she confirms rather than lightens the terrible imprint of Esther's childhood and reinforces her daughter's view that she brings 'calamity and disgrace on the house'. At the end, however, Lady Dedlock appears to attempt to make some amends for this harshness. We see her, at the bricklayer's hovel, asking about Esther's whereabouts when she fails to find her at Bleak House and she sends Esther a letter which eventually leads to her discovery. In a change from the novel, she appears to be alive when she is found outside the graveyard and able to look, for a final time, on her daughter (fig. 19).

Nevertheless, these explanations and attempted reparations do not quite capture the enigmatic control which characterises Lady Dedlock. She is introduced early in the first episode, announcing a boredom which seems to be more existential than circumstantial and which is visually expressed through several shots, full-on and in profile, of her face at the window (for example, figs 30 and 37). This gives us a clue as to her character even before the mystery of her past life impinges on her or the audience. As with Esther, the camera continually explores her face but, like Tulkinghorn, her expression gives little away; even when a tear runs down her cheek, her stillness makes her seem curiously remote from her own crying (fig. 31).

She often observes the actions of others in silence and, when she speaks, her words can be opaque and misleading. But despite the emphasis on control she also takes risks in sending Tulkinghorn messages via Sir Leicester, visiting him privately at night and in hiring Jo to show her where her lover spent his last days. Sometimes her feelings remain unexplained; her attachment to Rosa hints at her continuing distress over the loss of her daughter but she allows herself only to be coolly affectionate rather than sentimental. But the gap between outward control and normally hidden inner feeling is exposed in moments of masochistic breakdown when, for instance, she weeps despairingly during her confession to Esther or when, in her guilt, she flees knowingly to her death. Gillian Anderson's

30. Lady Dedlock looking out of Chesney Wold

31. Lady Dedlock at the window, at the beginning of episode 9, in a series of shots which ends with her weeping

performance presents this melodramatic mix with precision. Her eyes, unlike Tulkinghorn's, continually betray her feelings, moving with unnerving brightness even when hidden behind a veil. But the stillness and composure in her face set her apart from the characters she appears with, whether it be the grouchy, elastic face of Timothy West or the quick movements of Burn Gorman. Confronted, in episode 6, with a series of revelations about Esther from Guppy she manages to keep control even after he leaves, only allowing herself to breathe out with a sigh the words she 'She lived.'

Part of the characterisation of Lady Dedlock is created for the audience by the association with other characters played by Anderson. Thus, for those who have seen *The House of Mirth*, Lily Bart has the same air of suppressed passion, the same willingness to take risks and an even more insecure social position. But more famously, Anderson brings with her attributes of Dana Scully, the FBI agent she played in *The X Files*: intelligent insight as well as the famous sceptical rationalism, which, in a reversal of gender expectations, the female agent was allowed to show in the series. All of this, for at least some of the audience, contributes to the icy calm with which Anderson portrays Lady Dedlock. But *The X Files* also links Anderson with the sense of mystery generated by its paranormal stories and which may carry over into her character in *Bleak House*. Other actors in the programme can also be connected with previous performances, most markedly Johnny Vegas, whose persona as a comedian lent a leering, semi-jocular strain to his characterisation of Krook, yielding praise for a performance so different from his usual stand-up appearances. Since good acting is one of the most valued features in classic adaptations, this casting against type foregrounded the fact of performance and was effective in this case. Given that DVD availability extends access to the serial well beyond its initial screenings, the capacity for an actor to generate connotations that work with or against the character can now arise at a later stage. Perhaps Alun Armstrong's interpretation of the potentially sinister Bucket (he does after all kidnap Jo, arrest George and try to serve a warrant on the dying Gridley) is now softened for many viewers by his appearance as the eccentric but good-hearted detective in the BBC's hugely popular *New Tricks* (2003–).

6 Settings

Setting has always been a particularly important feature of the classic serial. The aim of the serial is not just to tell a story but to create a convincing representation of the fictional world in which it is to take place. This is true for stories told in any visual medium but it has a particular resonance for classic adaptations. Unless the work has been updated or modernised, the setting also has to establish the existence of an imaginary yet physical place within a knowable, or at least recognisable, past. This is often achieved through the use of period detail, which triggers some of the characteristic pleasures of the classic serial, described by Caughie as taking 'pleasure in detail … a pleasure in profusion … a pleasure of observation'.[134] The effect of this on the visual organisation of the classic serial will be discussed in the next chapter. Here I want to discuss how the settings are established visually and look at their contribution to our understanding of the narrative and characters. We could indeed see setting as being a particularly important element for *Bleak House* since the book is named after a place rather than a character. The title echoes other much-adapted, nineteenth-century classics with evocative place names – *Northanger Abbey* (1818) and *Wuthering Heights* (1847) – but more prosaically in 2005 it could be seen as having similarities with the titles of British soap operas which specifically reference the places where their characters live – *EastEnders*, *Coronation Street*, *Emmerdale*.

Audience interest in settings is now well known and, as a consequence, DVD commentaries often relay information about how

particular settings were dressed and shot; organisations like the
National Trust promote visits to their properties with articles about
their use as locations for television and film adaptations. The press
material for *Bleak House* (2005) provided precisely this kind of
information, explaining that the team was able to use Balls Park, a
Grade 1 listed building within easy reach of London, for a number of
different interiors while exteriors were filmed at other named houses.
Cobham Hall in Kent, for instance, served for the exterior of Chesney
Wold, allowing Stafford-Clark to claim, as semi-serious evidence of
authenticity, that 'Dickens used to walk to a pub in Cobham through the
very grounds of Cobham Hall where we filmed'. The press pack also
explains that 'the bustling 19th century streets of London' were created
by building a set around a cobbled stable block found at Luton Hoo,
Bedfordshire. Such a set was a reminder of the kind of large, standing set
constructed over the years for *EastEnders* and Stafford-Clark described
it to a journalist as 'our Albert Square'[135] but he was also keen to
emphasise that this was an economic way of working: 'Using the stable
block meant that we could use a set that was twice the size of anything
else we could have afforded to build from scratch.' In the DVD
commentary for episode 1, Justin Chadwick stresses that it was really
important to get the 'the feeling of London ... so difficult to do ... so
little of it exists any more'.

The 'bustling 19th century streets of London' make up one of
the most specific and popular images associated with Dickens. Indeed,
the effect of so many Dickens adaptations has been to create a rather
fixed image of Victorian London, with bustling streets and shops,
overhanging windows and cobbled passageways, peopled by Cockney
street vendors and theatrically dirtied children, with the darkness
pushed away into dens and passageways and the whole picture
overshadowed by the silhouette of St Paul's Cathedral. The
predominance of this image does indeed relate to the importance of
London in Dickens's novels. The city is, as Slater notes, 'the main setting
for – and in a sense the main character in – most of his writings' and
Ackroyd specifically sees 'the city as the mystery' which is 'at the heart

80

of *Bleak House*'.[136] But Dickens was recording a city that was far from
fixed, writing his novels in a period when London was 'more excavated,
more cut about, more rebuilt and more extended than at any time in its
previous history'.[137] In terms of remembering that London was
constantly changing, it is worth noting that one of the debates about
Bleak House, which Dickens vigorously defended, centred on how up
to date it was and whether Dickens, in 1852/3, was condemning, in
his depiction of Chancery and Tom-All-Alone's, a legal system and
sanitation practices which were already in the process of being
reformed. Finally, although Dickens knew London intimately, his
feelings towards it were not unambiguous; he spent much time living
elsewhere, particularly in Kent and France, in part to escape what he
called in a letter in 1851, the year before *Bleak House* started appearing,
'a vile place … . Whenever I come back from the Country, now, and see
that great canopy lowering over the housetops, I wonder what on earth I
do there, except on obligation.'[138] The representation of London is
therefore an important element in this adaptation but it is not the only
setting in *Bleak House* and this chapter will also look at the other two
main sites in the serial, the houses outside London: Bleak House itself
and Chesney Wold. In each case, I want to look at their distinctive
features and the way they support the narrative and characterisation.

 Bleak House (2005) denies the viewer a glimpse of London's
landmark features – St Paul's, for instance, or the Thames – which
would establish it visually as London.[139] Nor, despite the fact that we
start with Esther's journey into the city do we get the kind of view
common in *Oliver Twist* adaptations, of London viewed as a great
metropolis from afar. This is London viewed in close-up via a handheld
camera; following the characters, we catch glimpses of mud and
cobbles, bleached-out wooden signs and torn handbills, discarded
furniture, washing on the line, piles of baskets, wheels and hand carts. In
its attempt to immerse the audience in the experience of a nineteenth-
century city, *Bleak House* offers a dynamically growing London through
a setting which is more like that of *Deadwood* (2004–6) than some of
the more sanitised streets of tea-time adaptations.

81

This version of London depends on a complex set with a markedly permeable version of public and private space. The street is a public space where unrecognised connections can be made and missed and watchers can observe without being challenged. Esther literally bumps into her unknown father the moment she arrives there and, in episode 3, Tulkinghorn unknowingly raises his hat to a veiled Lady Dedlock. Hortense in the shadows observes the comings and goings at the grand town houses while Guppy stands quite openly in the street, looking up to strange windows in order to catch a glimpse of Esther. The openness of the street is tied to the image of London as a place of work, which means that, even off the street, people have to be available to each other and in some sense on display. The London setting takes in a range of semi-private spaces which are in fact open for business. Most of these spaces are connected to the law, cramped offices which are overflowing with paper. When Richard is apprenticed to Kenge and Carboy's, in episode 4, he is advised that the law is a matter of reading and, as he moves towards his desk, bundles of legal papers, leatherbound books and wooden filing boxes appear on the shelves behind him (fig. 32). Similarly, in episode 9, when Vholes assures Richard that 'we are very active [in pursuit of his case] ... no stone is left unturned', the packages of legal papers and the books piled up on the shelves around the office indicate the true state of things and, when Ada visits his office, in episode 12, Vholes peers at her through the legal papers piled up in columns of bundles on his desk. These offices are thus open and accessible to the lawyers' clients but, in their chaos and disorder, they physically represent the blockages in the system.

The grandest of these legal spaces is the Court of Chancery where the law can literally be observed at work. The main space, a central well, often filmed from above, holds the main players in the court; the Chancellor (Ian Richardson) is seated high above the layers of lawyers beneath him, their desks set against the black-and-white floor. Round them crowd the host of applicants, helpless but drawn there by the possibility that their case might break through into the court's business. The collapse of the Jarndyce case will be visually represented

32. Richard, fresh and hopeful, in the legal office

83

33. The papers fly up in the Court of Chancery as the Jarndyce case collapses

in a high shot of the court as legal papers fly up into the air (fig. 33). The jumble of lawyers and piles of papers in Chancery indicates its responsibility for obfuscation and delay and finds its counterpart in Krook's rag-and-bottle shop. Krook parallels the Chancellor as, sunk down in this lair, he attempts to police what is in effect a curious combination of thoroughfare to the upper rooms where his lodgers live and a jumbled archive of piles of untraceable papers. Chancery and Krook's shop are places which offer people some access to the hope that order can be restored and lives untangled but in both places obfuscation reigns.

The permeability of work spaces is reflected in how often characters are shown living in their workplaces. Krook lives in his shop and Tulkinghorn seems to live in the grand house which serves as his office while the Turveydrops live above the dance school. And Mrs Jellaby's kitchen is not a domestic space but the office through which she attempts to organise charitable works in Africa. George and Phil live in their working space, which is, however, markedly different from the cluttered legal offices. The shooting gallery has larger, high-ceilinged rooms, wooden floors and brick walls along which the straw shooting targets are symmetrically lined (fig. 34). George's business makes his home a public place and, although he offers it as a hiding place to the dying Gridley and a rough refuge for Jo, its privacy is breached by Bucket and Smallweed, who both invoke the law to grant them access.

George's shooting gallery is, nevertheless, the one working place in London which shows signs of vigorous activity taking place. We see Richard, learning to use a sword, in a sharp series of exchanges

34. George and Phil at the gallery

35. George and his gun

with George and, on several occasions, the physically powerful George
is framed to show him wielding a sword, whirling a set of clubs or lining
up his gun as if to fire (fig. 35). George's vigour functions to indicate
that he might be a threat to the legal and financial system which has
trapped him. But George finds his capacity for action is powerless
against the mental agility of Tulkinghorn and the imperturbable façade
of Inspector Bucket. In the windowless, boxlike gym there is a sense of
him turning this potential violence against himself.

     This representation of London is built up by moving the
viewer, like the characters, through a series of settings which only
gradually make sense in terms of their connections with particular
characters and themes. There are limits to how far the geography of the
serial's London can be established in a limited number of episodes
compared with the familiarity of, for instance, Albert Square after years
of soap viewing. But its attention to realistic detail offers rewards to the
observant viewer by building up a physical sense of place which
underpins the narrative and makes characterisation more precise by
linking particular characters to appropriately resonant settings.

     If London is an overwhelmingly public space in which stories
and characters most readily interweave and connect, the two other main

85

36. Esther, Charley and Ada approach Chesney Wold

locations offer private, domestic spaces tied to particular stories and characters. Although the use of such historic houses is a feature of the traditional classic serial, in creating its houses *Bleak House* continues the immersive approach adopted in the treatment of London, thrusting the viewer into the setting rather than offering a distant view allowing us to admire their period detail. The shooting style generally follows the established pattern of the camera following the character so that the detail of the setting has to be picked up on the move. Although establishing shots are included to mark the transition to these country houses, the speed of the cutting and the nature of the shot curtail what can be seen and deny us the unimpeded view of the country house. A number of outdoor scenes do in passing show the houses more clearly but it is significant that, in one of the few shots which allows the viewer to contemplate the façade of Chesney Wold, the view is obscured by the branches of a cedar tree and accompanied by dialogue in which both Charley and Esther proclaim firmly that they would not want to live in such a house (fig. 36).

Although filmed in a similar style, the houses are used to create very different settings and hence to contribute different meanings to the processes of characterisation and narrative. Chesney Wold is presented as cold and empty. Cool blue and grey interiors reinforce the melancholy of the rain of Lincolnshire outside its windows. Its formal rooms have an air of decay and its elaborate decor and furniture speak of a past splendour which can no longer be sustained. There are no personal touches. Lady Dedlock's portrait, which hangs on the grand stairway, is for public display, in line with the family tradition, and her bedroom is decorated in the same ornate style; the bed is hung with swathes of fabric and two elaborate chandelier-style lamps stand on the small tables which frame the draped window. Sir Leicester fits naturally into these surroundings and is often seen sitting down looking at papers or dealing with some item of business. Our first view of the couple shows Lady Dedlock looking out of the window as Sir Leicester conducts the conversation while reading his paper in a distant chair (fig. 37). This composition within the setting serves to indicate the secrets and separation within their marriage reiterated in subsequent images such as the shot shown in fig. 38; both characters appear in the frame but the fragility of the glass objects indicates their isolation within the marriage.[140] The first image of the figure of Lady Dedlock, rigid with boredom as she watches the rain fall over the Lincolnshire estate, becomes a consistent motif and allows us to witness her changing moods. It is repeated for instance at the opening

87

37. Lady Dedlock looks out into the rain while Sir Leicester reads

38. The Dedlocks in their self-enclosed bubbles at Chesney Wold

of episode 9 when the close-up of her face with a tear on her cheek (fig. 31) refers us back to her revelatory conversation with Esther in the previous episode; and again, in the first few seconds of episode 10, when shots of her deep in thought introduce the scene in which she will let Rosa go (fig. 30). Despite her claims to Tulkinghorn that she runs the house, the repetition of this image of her frozen in the attitude of looking out indicates that she is trapped there. This is a patriarchal household in which Sir Leicester's periodic fits of anger have the power to control the people within it.

It is a feature of this house that conversations are not sociable, shared events but conducted between two people in private spaces – the bedroom, the kitchen, hidden corridors. Lady Dedlock's bedroom hosts a number of these duologues. It is there that Mrs Rouncewell, without knowing that she's speaking of Lady Dedlock's daughter, tells her mistress about Esther's recovery from illness. The bedroom is also the setting for scenes with Rosa which illustrate Lady Dedlock's growing feeling for her maid as a substitute daughter and her reluctant decision to let her go. But her most secret conversations are with Tulkinghorn. Three of these take place at Chesney Wold: the first in a small private room where Tulkinghorn has eaten his solitary supper; the second in a shabby private room, which Lady Dedlock reaches by a backstairs corridor; and the third in the kitchen, after Lady Dedlock has broken up an apparently chance meeting between Rosa and the lawyer there. In these relatively enclosed and austere settings, the cutting alternately shows close-ups, often in antagonistic profile, of the faces of the two opponents so that, even in these small spaces, they hardly ever appear in the same frame (figs 39 and 40). Setting these scenes in the secret spaces

39 and 40. Tulkinghorn and ... Lady Dedlock confront each other

of a private house, like boxes within a box, underlines how Lady Dedlock exploits the physical fabric of Chesney Wold to maintain the secrets she hides from her husband and reinforces the sense of the catastrophe that will occur when she is forced out into the open.

The fact that Tulkinghorn eats his supper alone and that Sir Leicester and Lady Dedlock are never seen sharing a meal illustrates the difference between Chesney Wold and Bleak House. Despite its name, Bleak House opens itself up to guests and shared meals feature frequently in its representation. It is located outside London near St Albans but is accessible to the London characters. Richard, Esther and Ada are warmly welcomed there in episode 1 and other visitors, invited and uninvited, include those normally firmly ensconced in London, such as Miss Flite and Mr Vholes, as well as those from elsewhere, such as Mr Boythorn and Mrs Woodcourt. As with the other settings, although the décor is detailed and significant, it is not dwelt on for its own sake nor are particular objects or pieces of furniture signalled out for our appreciation by the *mise en scène*. Unlike Chesney Wold, Bleak House is decorated in a comfortable style with patterned wallpaper, pictures and mementoes on the walls, swathes of light fabric on tables and at windows, comfortable chairs and polished tables. The lighting is warm and bright, with rooms often lit with the glow of candles. There are private spaces in this domestic setting but Ada and Esther freely visit each other's bedrooms (on one such visit Ada delightedly finds Esther pressing Woodcourt's flowers) and Esther is a regular and welcome visitor in Jarndyce's refuge in the Growlery. Although Jarndyce is the owner of the house, this is a feminine household as is evident not only in the formal handing over of the keys to Esther by the female servant but also in its informality and the freedom with which Ada and Esther occupy its spaces.

Bleak House inhabitants are regularly represented enjoying sociable conversation and exchange at mealtimes. The framing and editing of these meal sequences show how they serve to bring the characters together in a group but also map out the variety of relationships within it. Characters are linked by being positioned in the same frame or by cutting from face to face with the flow of the conversation. Thus, the first meal in episode 1 starts with an establishing shot of the group with Jarndyce at the head and then 'falsely' pairs Richard and Esther in the same frame. Most of the shots, though, show a single character in close-up, reflecting the fact that key relationships have yet to be established. In episode 6, Esther and Ada are paired in a series of shots showing their alliance against Mrs Woodcourt while, in episode 8, the balanced cutting between Esther, Jarndyce and Ada at breakfast confirms that they are indeed the 'little circle' of which Esther speaks (fig. 41). At a subsequent breakfast, though, after Esther has accepted Jarndyce's marriage proposal, the new couple share the frame in a number of shots while Ada is now isolated. And, in episode 12, Ada's birthday is celebrated at their London home with a tense meal in which Ada's mediating position is confirmed by the way she is framed both with and between Richard and Jarndyce (fig. 42). The freedom in speech and looks and the visual framing of significant relationships in the filming of meals extends into other settings when the Bleak House inhabitants eat elsewhere. Thus, dinner in the Bayham Badgers household in episode 2 frames Richard and Ada and Esther and Woodcourt as prospective couples, leaving Jarndyce isolated; the dinner in Deal similarly sets up the

91

41. Breakfast at Bleak House

42. Ada mediates between Richard and Jarndyce at her birthday dinner

two couples separately in shots alternating with framing shots of the whole table which exemplify the loyalty of all four 'to friendship'.

This is not to say that Bleak House does not have its secrets. But, while Chesney Wold is constructed around secret locations, the open doors, central staircase and greater freedom of Bleak House work to bring together those at risk of misunderstanding their true relationships. The geography permits secrets but the characters generally respond with respect to each other. Thus, on entering Ada's bedroom in episode 6, Esther sees her hide a letter from Richard at the very moment she denies receiving it; in response, Esther ruefully accepts Ada's denial and waits to be told more. Similarly, in episode 8, Jarndyce, through an open door, overhears Esther revealing her feelings to Ada about the way in which smallpox has changed her looks. Later, Jarndyce responds by telling Esther directly that he has heard her fears and is 'sad to hear you talk the way you did'. And most crucially, in the final episode, it is the fact that Jarndyce overhears Esther's passionate crying through her bedroom door that leads to his resolution of the whole story by withdrawing his claim on her. Thus, the fabric of the house works with the behaviour of its occupants to mitigate the effect of secrets which threaten the intimacy of the household.

The other less prominent settings tend to share the features of the three main locations. The décor of the Dedlock London town house is less dominated by the family history but it has the same air of formality as Chesney Wold. Boythorn's house shares many of the comfortable characteristics of Bleak House itself and his guests appear settled and at home there; other middle-class houses like the Bayham Badgers' have a similar air. But other settings in the serial are linked to what Jeremy Tambling calls the novel's 'concern with wasted places'.[141] Key among these are Tom-All-Alone's, the graveyard and the Ghost Walk, places which exemplify the ultimate consequences of the

43. 'Tom-All-Alone's' by Phiz, scanned image by George P. Landow, <www.victorianweb. orgartillustration phizbleakhouse29. html>

93

44. Bucket seeks for those who are lost, at Tom-All-Alone's

frustration and obfuscation characterising the legal system and provide metaphors of the descent into disintegration and death. I would argue that these settings are less successfully depicted than the three principal locations. They are spaces which are meant to shock or frighten us but they also need to have a resonant, symbolic value, as Chesney Wold and Bleak House do, in terms of the programme's overall themes.

Tom-All-Alone's is the place to which the poorest and most desperate in society sink; Jo tries to hide there and Bucket takes Esther there in the search for Lady Dedlock before they descend further into disintegration by inspecting the drowned bodies dredged from the Thames. Tom-All-Alone's is represented as a small, underground room, very different from Phiz's original illustration (fig 43), in which derelict people are huddled, some in groups; it lacks alleyways or upper stories and its hiding places are readily opened up. The décor can be seen in some (relatively) long shots and the experience is represented largely through the viewpoints of the middle-class characters Bucket and Esther rather than Jo (fig. 44). It provides a bleak place of shelter and, despite the murky mist, this Tom-All-Alone's seems too solid, contained and coherent to indicate a place where human connections fail.

The same is true of the graveyard, which Hillis Miller describes as 'the center of anonymity, putrefaction and formlessness',[142] the place to which the doomed Lady Dedlock is inevitably drawn. But, at Nemo's pauper's burial, there is no attempt to show the graveyard as overcrowded with barely buried bodies; instead, the site offers a brief glimpse of the natural world, with shots of muddy grass and twigs against brick walls. A more atmospheric sense of place is created in episode 3 when Jo shows Lady Dedlock where Nemo was buried. A series of shots puts the viewer inside the iron railings surrounding the graveyard, giving an overall view of bluish mist, bare trees, skewed crosses and rats scurrying across the ground (fig. 45). But this is a rather generalised account based on horror conventions and lacks the precision of the dialogue between two people who cannot understand each other:

> Lady Dedlock: Is this consecrated ground? … Is it blessed?
> Jo: Don't know. But it ain't done it much good if it is.

95

Finally, at the end of episode 14, the emphasis is on Esther's sad reunion with her mother and the visual image of the graveyard is confined

45. Lady Dedlock and Jo at the graveyard

to the railings of the gate (fig. 20). Although this is effective in terms of Esther's story, the symbolic significance of the graveyard as the place of final degradation receives limited expression.

It seems likely that *Bleak House* paid a price for its pre-watershed scheduling and had to be careful not to create images of these disturbing places which might be deemed too powerful for younger audience members. But the same caution could not really be said to apply to the Ghost Walk. The serial seeks to maximise the atmospheric potential of the meeting at which Lady Dedlock reveals herself to be Esther's mother by transferring the encounter to the Ghost Walk, a liminal space between the formal gardens and the house itself. Earlier in the episode Esther had heard about the ghost of the dead wife who walks there and the well-lit, verdant setting has an air of picturesque ruin (fig. 46). But as the scene progresses the ominous qualities of the Ghost Walk recede in the face of the present-day drama between mother and daughter. In part, this is a consequence of the serial's focus on a clear narrative line but it is also due to its inability to establish the Ghost Walk more generally in the serial 'as an omen we are never allowed to forget' (Storey, 1987, p. 26). Rather than foreshadowing it earlier in the serial, the significance of this setting is largely confined to this episode

46. Esther and Lady Dedlock in the Ghost Walk

and the tale of the ghostly wife, whose footsteps presage the doom of the Dedlock family, is incongruously told by the bluff Boythorn, whose commonsense turns it into an amusingly scary tale for Ada and Esther.

In representing these settings, *Bleak House* might have done better to continue to rely on the visual organisation which marks the serial as a whole, blurring the image and surrounding the key elements with shadow and darkness. Instead, these three 'wasted spaces' seem too concrete, making it difficult for the viewer to feel symbolic connections between what is being shown on screen and its deeper significance for the story. This relates to a difficulty the serial has in making connections between its main settings in order to highlight the complex interrelationship between social, legal and family institutions which the novel powerfully suggests. The connections are made narratively through the Jarndyce case and the unravelling of the mystery of Esther's identity but the distinctive weight and dominance of the main settings make it difficult for the journeys that connect them – Jo's travels and Lady Dedlock's flight – to carry the metaphor of links being made between different levels of Victorian society. Jo, who is moved on between London and St Albans and back again, is the main narrative connection, accused of infecting Esther with the disease he carries from Tom-All-Alone's but, while the journey works to carry the story forward, its effectiveness as a metaphor 'for the unifying theme of infection, both physical and moral' at all levels of society is limited.[143] Similarly, Lady Dedlock's final flight helps to resolve the mystery but is too compressed to communicate her symbolic status as a scapegoat for sexual guilt. Dickens's mems indicate her panic – '"My enemy alive and dead" – Hunted, she flies' (Stone, 1987, p. 239) – and in the book this is given full expression. Her flight consists of two journeys, the first out of London and then back again to its morbid centre in the graveyard. In *Bleak House* (2005), she takes a single journey from Chesney Wold to London which seems more rational and lacks the compulsive repetition and doubling of the book.

This version of *Bleak House* notoriously dispensed with the book's great connecting metaphor of the fog, an omission which I will discuss in the next chapter, and its lack of such a controlling metaphor perhaps hampered its use of settings as omens or symbols. Nevertheless, there are considerable successes in the handling of the settings and they contribute much to the overall effect of the serial. *Bleak House* successfully avoids the fetishisation of décor which is a feature of many classic serials and its use of soap-opera techniques helps to create a geographically plausible setting for London which provides a physical equivalent of the interweaving storylines and chance encounters which mark the plot. More generally, the interplay of setting and *mise en scène* in the filming of the three main locations shows how they function to lend a physical form to the relationships of those who live or work within them. In continually linking characterisation and setting to show how the characters gain significance from the way they are positioned in and relate to their environment, *Bleak House* (2005) pays attention to one of the novel's great themes.

7 'Illustrating' *Bleak House*

In this final chapter, I want to look at the discussion of the visual organisation associated with this version of *Bleak House*, also taking in the reception of the serial by journalists and academics. It will, I hope, be clear that the visual dimension of the serial is crucial to the analysis of narrative, characterisation and setting. My account of those elements cannot be separated from the visual register since it does not transmit a previously established meaning but creates that meaning through viewing. Nevertheless, the relationship between the visual organisation of an adaptation and the telling of the story is often the subject of comment and this was particularly the case with *Bleak House*. In this chapter, rather than myself isolate visual organisation as a further element of analysis, I want to look at how the visual register has been isolated in the debate provoked by the serial and analyse the different ways in which practitioners and critics attempt to establish a discourse on this aspect. I am suggesting that the organisation of images in *Bleak House* has had a separate status in the discussion of the programme and that analysing that discussion helps to tease out some of the issues of adaptation at stake in its reception.

Separating the image from other elements in examining film and television texts has a particular resonance with regard to adaptations. A persistent, commonsense assumption about adaptations is that novels rely on words and films on images and indeed one of

Davies's rules of adaptation refers to this distinction: 'Never use a line of dialogue if you can achieve the effect with a look.'[144] In other words, if you can, it is better to reduce the dialogue and rely on images rather than words when writing a script for an adaptation. Such an approach is based on ideas about medium specificity which dictate that visual media such as film and television best communicate meaning and emotion through particular ways of using images. But taken too literally, the separation of words and images in this way, and the assumption that images communicate better, or at least more appropriately, than words, gives the impression that images operate as a layer which can be added on once the essence of what is being adapted or the effect needed has been identified.

The separation of word and image seems particularly inappropriate in the case of Dickens, for whom picturing the scenes he was writing was part of his creative process. 'I don't invent it – really I do not – but see it and write it down' he wrote to John Forster[145] and Ackroyd remarks of his creative process that pictures

> are more significant to him than ideas or themes or even, sometimes, words. He talks of his fiction on occasions as a 'picture-frame' but his pictures within the frame are not like the still lives of an artist; Dickens sees objects and images as if they had suddenly been illuminated by lightning.[146]

And of course Dickens has been one of the novelists most famously linked to the development of cinema, not just by Eisenstein in his discussion of montage, but in analysis of his writing, which notes 'how language seems to track dissolve, pan, cut – ... to anticipate those qualities which are so characteristic of film's continuous movements through time'.[147] In terms of television, John Romano, a screenwriter who worked on shows like *Hill Street Blues* (1981–7), picks out Dickens's eye for detail, his 'imperative to render ... the unfamiliar aspect of everyday things', as one of the reasons why 'Dickens stands over my shoulder as I write'.[148]

47. Title plates by Phiz from *Bleak House* (1853), scanned image by George P. Landow, <www.victorianweb. orgartillustration phizbleakhouse29. htm>

In addition, illustrations were an important element of Dickens's novels and provided information and atmosphere in a way that modern readers have lost sight of, even when the original illustrations are reproduced in the text. For readers of the serial, the wrapper cover, which was the same for each number, supplied 'a visual summary of the novel's thematic concerns' while the two plates each month 'helped to establish the identity and mark the development of Dickens's characters, the sequences of his plots, and the nature of his themes'.[149] The two plates could also indicate the story's range in each number by taking different kinds of characters and stories for their subjects. In the subsequent book version, illustrations could comment on each other as well as the text, as is seen in this example from the 1853 *Bleak House* in which the etching of Chesney Wold conveying 'loneliness, sterility, the lack of human connection' is set against the system's human cost represented by Jo (fig. 47).[150] The illustrations furnished by Hablot Browne in *Bleak House* changed markedly as the serial progressed; the dark plates of the final third of the book focused on the Dedlock story, showing few human figures and evoking 'oppression, confusion, and the power of dehumanized institutions' in etchings that detail the degradation of Tom-All-Alone's (fig. 43) and the

101

48. 'The Ghost Walk' by Phiz,   49. 'The Morning' by Phiz, scanned
scanned image by George P. Landow,   image by George P. Landow,
<www.victorianweb.orgartillustration <www.victorianweb.orgartillustration
phizbleakhouse29.htm>   phizbleakhouse29.htm>

gloomy splendour of the Ghost Walk (fig. 48).[151] The illustrations offer
a potentially influential source to adapters. Hunter has noted how, in
the 1985 *Bleak House*, Esther is often caught with her face averted or
obscured as she is in Browne's illustrations[152] and the high railings of the
graveyard gate before which the body of Lady Dedlock lies abased in
'The Morning' are a strong feature of the same scene in *Bleak House*
(2005) (figs 20 and 49). As with adaptations, there are debates about
whether illustrations should accurately reflect the written text. Steig
defends Browne's work from such criticism by arguing that an
illustration 'may present a point of view and bring out aspects which are
not overtly expressed in the text'[153] just as Andrew Davies argues that he
is offering an interpretation or a reading of the novel in his script.

We saw in Chapter 2 how the classic serial has changed over
the years but it is worth looking at these changes again in terms of the
genre's patterns of visual organisation. Sarah Cardwell argues that the

conditions of early television had an impact on the classic serial up until the 1970s: 'the combination of relatively still cameras, infrequent changes of *mise-en-scene* and lack of post-production editing led to an aesthetic which we would consider today staid and rigid'.[154] This restrained visual register was accompanied by an emphasis on the importance of the spoken word linked to the adaptations' function of educating the British viewer; adaptations were a way of introducing the public to great books and that required respect for their language. This context had the effect, according to Cardwell, of institutionalising a particular attitude to the medium of television in classic adaptations, a preference that 'the medium itself remain invisible, or at least transparent', as if the audience could look through the screen to the original source.[155] This began to change in the 1980s, when the influence of 'heritage cinema', often made with television money, encouraged a greater visual richness in photographing landscape and setting. Even so, in the 1990s, MacKillop and Platt, taking Davies's *Middlemarch* (1994) as their example, could still identify the classic novel television serial as a 'special television mode', 'committed to a literal respect for the original' with limited visual resources.[156]

103

But the television landscape had changed and increasingly in the 1980s and 1990s television drama was claiming a 'televisuality' based precisely on enjoyment of the medium's visual inventiveness by practitioners and audiences. In defining the term, John T. Caldwell identified a shift in mass-market US television from 'broadcasting primarily as a form of word-based rhetoric and transmission' to a 'visually based mythology, framework and aesthetic based on an extreme self-consciousness of style'.[157] Increasingly, style was upfront, designed to be noticed and enjoyed, the experience itself, not just something to support the content. And, although television drama was by no means the main plank of his argument, televisuality was to be found, not only in artistic dramas aimed at a specialist audience, but in popular television series such as *Hill St Blues* and *Miami Vice* (1984–90).

This interest in style as to-be-looked-at rather than to-be-looked-through was a challenge to the classic serial's more conservative tendencies throughout the 1990s. In some senses, though, debates about adaptations already had a tendency to see at least certain Dickens's novels as requiring a different form of adaptation. Smith, criticising Christine Edzard's 1988 film of *Little Dorrit*, argues that 'aesthetically, Dickens's work is the reverse of the art that modestly conceals itself' and that adaptations therefore have to find some way of embodying the novels' 'self-reflexive attention to themselves as created works of fiction'.[158] Cardwell suggests that Dickens adaptations 'have generally … rejected straightforward naturalism, bringing out the expressionistic qualities of the sources' though Giddings, while supporting the call for greater attention to style, is still of the view that 'British TV versions of Dickens err on the side of worthy, social realism'.[159] One interesting example of this call for Dickens adaptations to move away from transparency is Jefferson Hunter's praise for the moments in *Bleak House* (1985) which 'prefer stylization to naturalism and a powerful cinematic rhetoric to understatement'.[160] Hunter's use of the term 'cinematic' to praise a television adaptation reflects a widespread tendency to see visual complexity or pleasure as a cinematic property. Twenty years later *Bleak House* (2005) offered a challenge to that assumption.

By the 2000s, as we saw in Chapter 1, it was clear that classic serials had moved decisively away from visuals concentrating either on transmission of the source or, in heritage mode, on transmission of the landscape and were becoming 'stylistically more innovative, varied and reflexive'.[161] And certainly the makers of *Bleak House* (2005) were looking to be part of that movement. We saw in Chapter 2 how the production team emphasised advanced technology and contemporary drama as key influences on their work for *Bleak House* and their discussion of the visual register of the serial reflects this. Their commentary focused on two technological innovations – HD and the 'breathing camera'. Shooting in HD was still a relatively rare phenomenon for British television and in 2005 there was no provision for HD transmission in the UK. But it was becoming a requirement for US co-productions – *Planet Earth* (BBC, 2006) was another example –

and there was much interest at this point in the production of HD content. The BBC production diary has Stafford-Clark comment on the topic by telling a story about Kieran McGuigan, the director of photography on the shoot: 'HD made most DOPs very nervous. No-one had used it for a period show, and no-one knew how it would look. "Let's find out" said Kieran, beaming.'

In July 2005 McGuigan was featured in a special edition of the industry magazine *Broadcast* which used *Bleak House* as one of a number of HD case studies; in the interview, he emphasised his desire to keep control of the visuals rather than hand them over to the post-production process:

'People say that with digital cameras you should shoot it wide open, keep it flat and then bring it to life in the grade during the post-production process – but I don't want to have a little man in a telecine suite controlling the images,' he says. 'It goes against the grain to leave it to someone else.'

In his account, McGuigan says that he concentrated in particular on the colour palette, using his grading box to 'put in some greens, add some yellow and crunch the blacks' and adds that he was able to play with the exposure to create an emotional effect:

For instance, when someone walked towards a window, I would squeeze it down a bit and then move into more of a silhouette sort of feel and, as the character comes out through the shadows again, I'd open it up a bit to create an emotional narrative to the movement of the medium. I knew that if I left it to the grade, this sort of information wouldn't be there.[162]

This emphasis on an emotional engagement with the visuals is also a feature of the DVD commentary when it turns to the use of HD. In commenting on episode 1, Justin Chadwick talks about how the detail of HD was embraced right across the craft skills and of its enhancement of the immediacy of the visual register: 'You're absolutely in there with these actors, these performers, with this world' he comments and, when

Stafford-Clark remarks on how HD emphasises the expressiveness of
the eyes, he responds with 'Yes, you could just reach in and touch the
close-ups.'

The other publicised technical feature is also associated with
making the visuals more intimate. Shooting on the serial involved the
simultaneous use of two handheld cameras, which enabled a more fluid
handling of dialogue scenes since it removed the need to stop to set up
reaction shots. This mode of shooting also meant that dialogue scenes
could be rendered less static by adopting the unusual practice of cutting
immediately from a close-up of a speaking character to a close-up of the
same character from a different position. As part of this emphasis on
movement, the production team wanted an image that did not appear
unnaturally stable thanks to the use of a rock-steady Steadicam. Instead,
the image showed traces of the process of shooting. Stafford-Clark told
the press:

> It's what they now call breathing camera … . You notice very slight
> movements at the edge of the frame – it's the cameraman breathing – that
> gives it a feeling of tension that is absolutely right for this show. *Bleak
> House* is all about secrets withheld and divulged, and there is this
> tremendous emotional tension.[163]

By discussing, in detail, the technicalities of filming the adaptation,
and the emotional resonance they were trying to generate, production
team members were able to establish that their major concern was not
the traditional one of getting the period details right while allowing
the décor to be clearly seen. HD shooting and the 'breathing camera'
were augmented by a fast-paced style with swish pans and zooms,
ostentatious cuts and odd angles, extreme close-ups contrasted with
self-consciously picturesque long shots, all accompanied by a dense
soundtrack. The main character in a shot is often placed to one side
or in shadow and what we are looking at is frequently obscured by
positioning the camera behind the blurred traces of foliage, trellises,
railings, bars or shelves. The production team does not feel

constrained by the visual conventions of the classic serial and crucially it attempts to tie its use of technology to the generation of intimacy and emotion and an emphasis on rendering performance and feeling.[164]

We have seen how successfully the BBC press office introduced the idea that *Bleak House* was working in the same tradition of serialisation as Dickens. The same was not true of the reception of the visual style of the serial. The British press largely praised the adaptation but picked out the visual experiments for special treatment. In the *Independent*, Fiona Sturges did associate the 'twitchy editing and careening cameras' with 'a pleasingly contemporary edge'[165] but others found it more problematic. The viewer had to be recommended to get used to the style: 'The editing and camera work are fast and snappy, so initially it is quite hard to follow' as Paul Hoggart said in *The Times*.[166] Andrew Billen comments on 'the arty, fidgety camera work' without connecting it to modern edginess and John Mullan found that the visual style owed more to television fashion than Dickens, noting that 'what is most modish about this adaptation is the camera work'.[167] Mullan also commented on the gloom, finding that 'the darkness is obsessive'. This complaint was a common one and is possibly a problem associated with HD visuals being watched on non-HD equipment. 'At times it's so steeped in gloom that it's hard to work out just what is going on,' complained the *Sunday Telegraph* while Victor Lewis-Smith, although praising 'the use of colourising that changes from location to location', also commented on the 'all-encompassing gloom in the urban scenes'.[168] In *The Times*, Ian Johns gave an account which picks up on some of the references that the visual style was drawing on and adds some more of his own:

> At times it's like watching frames from a graphic novel with characters off-centre in a sea of black while scenes change and the camera moves to what sounds like an Imperial Starfighter swooping into battle. Imagine *Spooks* as a classic serial with the key plot details treated in the same zoom-in-quick manner as a threat to national security.[169]

Johns adds: 'I feel a little smothered by its style but I'm hooked' and, moving away from the visuals, goes on to admire 'Davies's tweaking of the characters and the strength of the performances'. This sense that the visual style requires some commentary but that the serial can be enjoyed despite rather than because of it is summarised in *The Times* TV guide, which recommended the serial by emphasising that the camera work is dispensable:

> Although it has been filmed using the edgiest of camera-work, the story is so engrossing and the acting so ripe that it could just as well be performed on a bare stage in modern dress without losing any of its impact.[170]

It could be argued that the BBC succeeded in linking visual style to innovation and a modern approach but failed to establish that as integral to the project.

The bulk of this television journalism, when it is not presenting prescreening publicity as many of these articles do, follows the common practice of aligning with the viewer and writing the review as a critique of the first episode, thus allowing the critic to formulate an immediate response much as the viewer does. While a few critics do occasionally revisit programmes during the rest of the run, it is rare for a television critic to respond at the end of a serialisation or series or to base their comments on much more knowledge than that available to the viewer at the time of reading. With an adaptation, though, the original source supplies another object for the critic and it is interesting, in relation to reviews of *Bleak House*, to note that a number of critics chose to share their prior knowledge of Dickens and the novel. It is also striking, even in the most upmarket papers, how many critics praise the serial by reassuring viewers that there is no need to have read the novel and set the pleasures of the television version against the alleged *longueurs* of the original as in the following examples:

> BBC1's *Bleak House* adaptation is a masterpiece – and all the more thrilling for so dramatically improving upon Dickens's rambling potboiler.

… Years ago, I remember struggling with the novel (I just thought, 'Oh, do get on with it!') but even at this early stage of Andrew Davies's 15-parter, it will be impossible not to go the distance.[171]

Most of *Bleak House*'s drawbacks were effectively dispensed with: the numbing weight of words, the drifts of often suffocating description and a storyline so meandering one could do with a map just to stay on course.[172]

Wisely acknowledging that the strange metaphoric life of Dickens's descriptions works only on the page, Andrew Davies's adaptation plunged straight into the labyrinthine plot … .[173]

The critics display their 'knowledge' of Dickens but do so in order to advise us that certain features of Dickens only work on the page and encourage us not to give up should the opening instalment prove confusing. So it is perhaps not surprising that relatively few critics went on to make a link between the serial's visual approach and the author's original as Simon Jenkins did:

109

I can dispense with fog which was, to Dickens, a literary metaphor … . The camera achieves the same claustrophobia with its nervy close-ups, dark sets and costumes and intense facial expressiveness. The pictures are fast and impressionistic. So is the novel. So was Dickens.[174]

This link between visual style and theme has been more common in academic analysis of *Bleak House* (2005) though, given the recent date of the production, such accounts have been relatively few. These critics, like the journalists, treat the visual organisation of the serial as a separate strand but seek to integrate it by making a connection between the visual style and Dickens's prose. In doing so, they raise the question commonly addressed in adaptation studies as to whether screen material can have the same kind of 'voice' – first person or third person – as novels and they try to find in the visual style of *Bleak House* the equivalent of Dickens's mode of narration. This means basing their judgment of the visuals not only on how they relate to the modern televisuality claimed by the BBC and the production team but also by comparing the adaptation to its source.

Such an approach is hinted at in Chris Louttit's comparison of *Bleak House* with the BBC's *Cranford* (2007). Louttit records that *Bleak House* was 'unconventional stylistically, marrying period drama with an MTV-influenced aesthetic' but he adopts a somewhat sceptical attitude to it, telling us that 'even arch-innovator Davies found' the shooting technique 'a touch gimmicky'. But Louttit does suggest that the camera work and editing

> might even be read as an innovation which is surprisingly Dickensian in manner, representing visually the unpredictable and often jarring shifts of tone that [have been] defined as a characteristic feature of Dickens's immensely performative narrative voice and prose style.[175]

This approach is pursued in more detail by others. Iris Kleinecke-Bates discusses the visual organisation of *Bleak House* (2005) in terms of the move away from the transparent realism of the traditional classic serial. She comments on the opening in which the familiar trappings of 'carriages, wet cobble-stones and costume' are undercut by 'fast and self-conscious editing' and which culminates in a sudden cut on a zoom to the High Court of Chancery. This, she suggests, is an example of the way the serial frustrates the viewer's 'desire to linger and see' and she goes on to argue that 'the adaptation responds to Dickens's prose in a visual way'.[176] John Caughie suggests a similar relationship between source and adaptation, arguing that 'there is in this television *Bleak House* a process of translation which replaces verbal mannerism with visual and aural density' and illustrating that the novel's complexity can be handled within the serial format: 'visually, the complexity is dramatized in the televisual rhetoric of swish pans and zooms; the three-shot pattern to establish a new location … a soundscape which gives expression and emphasis to the action rather than simply accompanying it'. In developing its own account of Dickens's world, the serial therefore draws on the 'visual language' of popular television drama so that a scene between Jarndyce and Esther is 'faithfully repeated in the adaptation' but is nevertheless understood differently by the audience because of the difference between Esther's first-person literary narration and the visual rendering of it in the adaptation.[177]

Rebecca Arwen White presents the most detailed account of the adaptation so far and the opening part of her analysis works to tease out further how the handling of camera work and *mise en scène* can equate to the organisation of narrative voice in the novel. She suggests, for instance, that the third-person narrator of the novel combines 'directorial comment with both the detail and the panoramic view of a camera lens'[178] and that this visual quality in Dickens's prose can in turn be rendered televisually. She argues that 'the dynamic pace' of the serial 'emulates and explores the novel's narrative form' and that 'the rapidity of camera movement intimates the "presentness" of the novel's omniscient voice'. Esther's voice is also rendered through the pace and virtuosity of the camera work; as the serial opens with Esther's journey in the coach to London, 'the frenetic energy of the camera, as it shakes and zooms, disturbs the viewer just as it visualises Esther's disorientated alienation'. White equates the ability of close-ups and zooms to pick out significant detail with the 'assured precision of an omniscient perspective' and suggests that Dickens's dual narrative is rendered through the 'constant merging of, and shift between, long shot and close-up'. In place of the novel's 'linguistic vibrancy', it is 'the ever-shifting camera angles' which challenge fixed conceptions of characters and theme while the heightened exaggerations communicated in Dickens's prose are, in the adaptation, made visible in the distortions generated by jumps, cuts and the use of the wide-angled lens. Thus, White in her detailed reading of the adaptation's visual register, is consistently concerned to relate it to Dickens's prose.[179]

It seems appropriate to condense the various positions by concluding with a comment about the fog, which became something of a benchmark for judgments about the serial. The great description of the fog which envelops the Chancery, the city and the country beyond is probably the most famous thing about the book (as Davies commented, 'I kept saying that the only thing people remember about *Bleak House* is that it's f***ing foggy'[180]) and contributed to a much more generalised image of Victorian London. It is a verbal rendering of a physical phenomenon which serves both to make everything obscure and to connect apparently separate parts. Its omission upset a number of commentators ,including novelist Philip Hensher, who prefaced his public assertion that he did not intend to watch the programme with 'For a start, I've heard that there is no fog to be seen anywhere …'.[181] But in fact the loss of the fog was by no means mourned by all. The production team made technical excuses about the fog effect being impossible to control when filming but this jettisoning of such a well-known reference (and particularly one which literally obscured the view) served to underline the team's commitment to a modern visual approach rooted in its own assessment of what made for good television. In the same way as Kieran McGuigan had worked to keep control of the HD 'look', so the absence of the foggy beginning indicated that Stafford-Clark and the directors had taken control of the 'look' of the serial and resisted any visual image imposed on them by the original text.

Quite a number of television reviewers were willing to go along with this approach and, in the flippant style that was depressingly common, the fog became something of a joke, a good launching point into a discussion of the serial. 'I tend to recall the mud and the fog, the squalor and the fog, the human suffering and … the fog' wrote Ian Johns while recognising that 'there is no time for reflection or a fog-shrouded London panorama here'.[182] Andrew Billen remarked that 'Instead of "fog everywhere", the meteorological conditions have worsened … . There is rain everywhere.'[183] These jokes about the novel's use of fog as a metaphor allow the reviewers to demonstrate their knowledge of (and implicitly their superiority to) Dickens. Such comments also allow them to show that they know that classic serials need no longer remain respectfully faithful to the source.

Academic critics too were willing to dispense with the physical fog but, as we have seen, they were less prepared to abandon its symbolic function. Caughie's argument that 'the mannerism of Dickens's allegorical invocation of the fog [at the beginning of the book] is replicated in a highly mannered visual rhetoric' is typical of this approach.[184] Kleinecke-Bates considered that the fog was an overused stereotype and that *Bleak House* was indeed adopting a new approach when it employed 'camera work and editing to convey the visual obstruction of the fog'.[185] Such critics seek to find a visual equivalence not just for the fog but for the whole verbal system of rhetoric that created it. In doing so, they adopt an approach which ties the adaption to the source much more fully than the makers might wish or the journalists might consider necessary. I shall pursue this further in the conclusion which follows.

Conclusion: Classic Television

This account of *Bleak House* appears in a series of books about 'television classics' but is it appropriate for such a recent programme to be assigned that status? It has already passed one test by appearing in a UK textbook for students taking their 16+ exams in English and Media Studies.[186] But it could just as soon fall out of the spotlight and it may indeed be harder for an adaptation to establish itself in its own right, rather than be seen as a version of a classic book to be overtaken by another in due course. It is interesting that, in the British Film Institute's list of television's top 100, seven of the top twenty serials/series were adapted from literature but that they tended to be one-offs such as *Brideshead Revisited* and *I, Claudius* (1976) rather than from the regularly adapted Austen, Brontë or Dickens.[187] We can therefore ask whether this is a *Bleak House* for the 2000s, a typical product of its time, or whether it has a chance of a longer life as a work that slips free from its specific context to be enjoyed by and speak to later generations?[188]

Bleak House can certainly be seen as a product of its time. The context created for the serial demonstrates in microcosm the strategies of scheduling and branding for the audience which the BBC feels is necessary for its quality drama and reveals much about the politics surrounding British public-service television broadcasting. As we have seen, the programme's publicity material encouraged viewers to see it as, among other things, a soap opera, a trailblazing modern television drama and an attempt to return Dickens to his popular audience. In a multi-channel environment, the publicity performed its basic task of highlighting the programme as important and letting viewers know that it was on 'after *EastEnders*'. But it also sought to brand the programme as generically mixed – a soap *and* a classic serial – and to associate it with some key BBC values: appeal to a popular audience; commitment to high-quality content; and the trailblazing of technical advances such as the use of HD. In the BBC of the 2000s, *Bleak House* could not be just a programme but became an element to be used by senior management in its strategic battles: 'we need to build fewer titles with longer runs, more impact, more emotion' said Mark Thompson, explaining the rules for drama in his 'Creative Futures' strategy, 'and make more brave calls like *Bleak House* and *Doctor Who*'.[189]

The 'natural' audience for a classic serial is generally considered to be those who know and love the genre and who are probably familiar with the book or at least might be inspired to read it. Thompson's link between *Doctor Who* and *Bleak House* was a controversial one because it challenged the traditional connotations of the classic serial by suggesting that it shared the same status and quality as a popular children's science-fiction drama. Even more irritating for some was the fact that, the more the literary establishment complained, the better it was for *Bleak House*, demonstrating definitively that this was indeed a different kind of adaptation, free from the fuddy-duddy restrictions of the classic serial genre. There is a danger that this contentious context will actually become what the programme is best known for and will deflect attention from analysis of the work itself. In writing this study, I found it sometimes difficult to see the programme stripped of all the hype, to disentangle it from the context that the BBC and the production team had provided. But the detailed analysis I was able to do here (and the programme would repay more) demonstrated that *Bleak House* deserves to be remembered as a television classic for other reasons.

As an adaptation, *Bleak House* takes on Dickens with a boldness which the author surely deserves. The range of the novel, the risks it takes in narration, theme and imagery, the inventive detail of its characterisation, its evocation of setting and environment and its powerful use of language, all deserve a response which is also bold, decisive and imaginative. This adaptation seemed to me to have the style, confidence and ambition to enable it to stand alongside the novel without attempting the impossible task of reproducing it faithfully. I believe it did establish a rewarding relationship with its source and it was a pleasure to find that some of the methods critics have used when analysing the novel were equally illuminating when brought to bear on the serial.

But a television classic should surely have its own status, rather than rely on its source for legitimacy. Otherwise the judgment of its merit relies on how well it functions as an adaptation, as Giddings suggested, when he praised the programme as 'something truly "Dickensian" … [and] true to the spirit of the original'.[190] But, to qualify as a television classic, an adaptation needs to be powerful and affecting in its own right and here I return to the argument developed at the end of Chapter 8. There we saw how *Bleak House*'s camera work and framings, its editing and use of sound were discussed by television scholars as the equivalent of the novel's fog (or more broadly of Dickens's prose). But that 'explanation' for the visual effects puts the emphasis on their function in relation to Dickens's original rather than on how the visual organisation might work with the other elements to give the programme its own distinctiveness. Similarly, the belief held by some journalists that overtly modish and derivative visual effects had been imposed on the story encourages the view that the visual style is a separate element which could be taken away or done differently without damaging the programme. In turn, the production team's referencing of visual elements from a long list of other programmes rather reinforced this notion of visual style as something that is separate and dispensable.

I would argue instead that *Bleak House*'s coherence depends on the establishment of a fully developed visual style which holds together the various settings, the huge cast of characters and the complications of the plot. On one level, it visually conveys some of the

116

key themes of the narrative: the obscured views and off-centre framings demonstrate the reliance of the characters on secrets and deceits; the editing links some characters and separates others; the lighting creates the mood and tone of a scene; and the framing and editing support some very fine performances. But I would also suggest that its strength lies in the way in which the visual organisation jolts the viewer, breaks up the clear narrative line established by the script and affords a different perspective.

We can see this in a range of examples. The speed and variation of the shots in the establishing montages consistently work against the traditional function of giving us a settled position from which to view the past (figs 50–2). Similarly, the use of a number of quick shots to show face and gesture when introducing characters or presenting them in key moments lends them a variation and complexity which they might not otherwise have, making Lady Dedlock, for instance, more fragile, Esther less secure and Krook more dangerous. The shooting in HD and McGuigan's 'crunching' of blacks creates a lighting scheme which can remove characters from context and melodramatically float the pale faces of Esther and Lady Dedlock against inky-dark backgrounds. Tight close-ups intensify our emotional engagement but, on other occasions, we are pushed back and characters diminish within the image, as we struggle to see Lady Dedlock disappear down a corridor, to identify Richard moving into the gloom of Kenge and Carboy's or make out George in the panelling of Tulkinghorn's office. Throughout *Bleak House* the images work not just because they are striking or beautiful, though they often are, but because they have an intricate relationship with narrative, setting and performance.

In developing this complex treatment of a complex story, the production demanded much of the audience and this was perhaps the real benefit from the comparisons with soap opera. Despite the nonsense about Dickens writing soaps, the serial benefited from the production team's confidence in the effectiveness of a popular form and its willingness to put faith in the inventiveness of contemporary television. Most classic serials are made with two audiences in mind – those who

117

50–2. A characteristic three-shot establishing sequence showing Bleak House

know the book and those who do not – but *Bleak House* committed itself to the latter, the supposedly ignorant audience. But it treated members of that audience as being expert at television and trusted them to make visual links, narrative connections and moral judgments about the programme. In that sense, *Bleak House* democratises the classic serial not by turning it into a soap but by exploring the possibilities of television in the same creatively engaging way as soaps, at their best, can do. But, as the critical history of Dickens's *Bleak House* shows, 'classics' do not emerge without a good deal of debate and disagreement. I hope that this book contributes to and extends that debate for *Bleak House* (2005).

Notes

1 Throughout this book, the title *Bleak House* may refer to the novel or the television versions and I will give the date when there is any ambiguity as to which I mean.

2 Grahame Smith, *Charles Dickens: A Literary Life* (Basingstoke: Macmillan, 1996), pp. 26–7. Smith's book is an invaluable and concise discussion of Dickens's writing and publishing practices.

3 Michael Slater, *Charles Dickens* (New Haven, CT, and London: Yale University Press, 2011), p. 239.

4 Smith, *Charles Dickens*, p. 161.

5 Ackroyd cited by Smith, *Charles Dickens*, p. 15.

6 Smith, *Charles Dickens*, p. 2.

7 Juliet John, *Dickens and Mass Culture* (Oxford: Oxford University Press, 2010), p. 49.

8 Slater, *Charles Dickens*, p. 137.

9 Peter Ackroyd, *Dickens* (London: Random House, 1991), p. 495.

10 Smith, *Charles Dickens*, p. 33.

11 Slater, *Charles Dickens*, p. 434.

12 Slater, *Charles Dickens*, p. 559.

13 Ackroyd, *Dickens*, p. 719.

14 Smith, *Charles Dickens*, p. 111.

15 Philip Hensher, 'You'll Never Catch Me Watching It', *Guardian*, 7 November 2005. Andrew Davies responded with an article 'Critical Dedlock', two days later.

16 See the introduction to Christine Geraghty, *Now a Major Motion Picture: Film Adaptations from Literature and Drama* (Lanham, MD: Rowman & Littlefield, 2008).

17 John Caughie, 'Television and Serial Fictions', in David Glover and Scott McCracken (eds), *The Cambridge Companion to Popular Fiction* (Cambridge: Cambridge University Press, 2012 forthcoming), p. 65.

18 Robert Giddings and Keith Selby, *The Classic Serial on Television and Radio* (Basingstoke: Palgrave, 2001), pp. 13, 19.

19 Jeffrey Richards, *Films and British National Identity: From Dickens to Dad's Army* (Manchester: Manchester University Press, 1997), p. 345.

20 Giddings and Selby, *The Classic Serial on Television and Radio*, p. 26.

21 Giddings and Selby, *The Classic Serial on Television and Radio*, p. 82.

22 Giddings and Selby, *The Classic Serial on Television and Radio*, p. 150.

23 Slater, *Charles Dickens*, p. 353.

24 Giddings and Selby, *The Classic Serial on Television and Radio*, p. 121.

25 Richards, *Films and British National Identity*, p. 345.

26 Giddings and Selby, *The Classic Serial on Television and Radio*, p. 75.

27 Jefferson Hunter, *English Filming, English Writing* (Bloomington: Indiana University Press, 2010), p. 170.

28 Michael Pointer, *Charles Dickens on the Screen* (London and Lanham, MD: Scarecrow Press, 1996), p. 96.

29 Quoted in Pointer, *Charles Dickens on the Screen*, p. 113.

30 Robin Nelson, *State of Play Contemporary 'High-End' TV Drama* (Manchester: Manchester University Press, 2007), p. 34.

31 Feuer, Jane, 'HBO and the Concept of Quality TV', in Janet McCabe and Kim Akass (eds), *Quality TV: Contemporary*

American Television and Beyond (London and New York: I. B. Tauris, 2007), p. 157.
32 For a comparison between *Bleak House* and *The Wire*, see Caroline Levine, 'From Genre to Form: A Response to Jason Mittell on *The Wire*' at www.electronicbookreview.com/thread/firstperson/serialrip. My thanks to Charlotte Brunsdon for this reference. Comparing the construction of *The Wire* to that of a novel has helped elevate its status and colour its reception.
33 Quoted in Stephen Armstrong, 'Under the Wire', *Media Guardian*, 6 April 2009, p. 3.
34 Christina Pishiris, 'Do It Like Dickens' *Televisual*, August 2005, p. 22.
35 The BBC press pack was released on 4 October 2005 and is still available at www.bbc.co.uk/pressoffice/pressreleases/stories/2005/10_october/04/bleak.shtml. All subsequent quotations ascribed to the press pack are taken from this source.
36 Quoted in Iris Kleinecke-Bates, 'Victorian Realities: Representations of the Victorian Age on 1990s British Television', PhD thesis (University of Warwick, 2006), p. 98. Kleinecke-Bates discusses both *The Forsyte Saga* and ITV's *Dr Zhivago* (2002; scripted by Davies) as examples of a new approach to the classic serial which predates *Bleak House*.
37 Fincham's speech is available at www.bbc.co.uk/pressoffice/pressreleases/stories/ 2005/07_july/14/bbc1.shtml.
38 Although the emphasis in the UK was on the thirty-minute scheduling, it was also shown in a weekly hour-long omnibus edition (like *EastEnders*). Elsewhere the serial was shown in longer episodes; in the US, for instance, it was shown on PBS in six parts in January/February 2006 and in four parts in 2007, illustrating the fact that the thirty-minute format made for a greater flexibility when it came to broadcast.
39 In this context, it is also significant that both the directors, Justin Chadwick and Susanna White, came with experience of popular drama with *Spooks* and *Teachers* (2001–4) respectively.
40 Quoted by Robert Giddings in 'Soft-soaping Dickens: Andrew Davies, BBC 1 and Bleak House', on David Purdue's Charles Dickens Page, www.charlesdickenspage.com/Soft_Soaping_Dickens.html. This interview took place in December 2004 and quotations from this article will subsequently be footnoted as Giddings, 'Soft-soaping Dickens'.
41 Deborah Cartmell and Imelda Whelehan, 'A Practical Understanding of Literature on Screen: Two Conversations with Andrew Davies', in Deborah Cartmell and Imelda Whelehan (eds), *The Cambridge Companion to Literature on Screen* (Cambridge: Cambridge University Press, 2007), p. 245.
42 The production diary was made available to viewers at www.bbc.co.uk/drama/bleakhouse/behindthescenes/production_diary_paginated_feature.shtml and subsequent quotations from it refer to this source.
43 All examples taken from the microfiche collection on *Bleak House* (2005) held at the BFI Library.
44 Mary Evans, *TV Times*, 25 November, 2005; David Butcher, *Radio Times*, 2 December 2005, p. 116. Both in microfiche collection at the BFI Library.
45 All figures from the trade journal *Broadcast*.
46 Overall figure from the Internet Movie Database.
47 See www.bbc.co.uk/pressoffice/speeches/stories/fincham_voice.shtml.
48 See www.bbc.co.uk/pressoffice/speeches/stories/thompson_fleming.shtml.

121

49 *The Late Show Who Framed Charles Dickens?* (BBC, 1994).

50 Giddings, 'Soft-soaping Dickens'.

51 Smith, *Charles Dickens*, p. 21.

52 Smith, *Charles Dickens*, p. 53.

53 See 'Preface' to *Bleak House* (New York: Norton & Co., 1977).

54 John Butt and Elizabeth Tillotson, *Dickens at Work* (London: Methuen, 1957), p. 14.

55 Butt and Tillotson, *Dickens at Work*, pp. 21–2.

56 Ackroyd, *Dickens*, p. 706.

57 John Forster, *The Life of Charles Dickens* (London: Dent, 1969), p. 120; Slater, *Charles Dickens*, p. 493.

58 Smith, *Charles Dickens*, p. 37.

59 Ackroyd, *Dickens*, p. 527.

60 Butt and Tillotson, *Dickens at Work*, p. 27.

61 Slater, *Charles Dickens*, p. 243. See Harry Stone (ed.), *Dickens' Working Notes for His Novels* (Chicago, IL: University of Chicago Press, 1987) for reproductions of the mems for *Bleak House*.

62 Smith, *Charles Dickens*, p. 12.

63 Slater, *Charles Dickens*, p. 511.

64 Smith, *Charles Dickens*, p. 10.

65 Slater, *Charles Dickens*, p. 344.

66 Smith, *Charles Dickens*, p. 111.

67 Reprinted in A. E. Dyson (ed.), *Dickens Bleak House: A Casebook* (London: Macmillan, 1969), p. 60.

68 From a review in *The Sun* reprinted in Philip Collins (ed.), *Dickens: The Critical Heritage* (London: Routledge & Kegan Paul, 1971), p. 228.

69 Reprinted in Dyson, *Dickens Bleak House*, pp. 56, 59.

70 *Prospective Review* reprinted in Collins, *Dickens*, p. 264.

71 Slater, *Charles Dickens*, p. 493.

72 Quoted in Ciar Byrne, 'What the Dickens! BBC Rebuilds "Bleak House" for the Hollyoaks Generation', *Independent*, 5 October 2005.

73 W. J. Harvey, '*Bleak House*: The Double Narrative' in Dyson, *Dickens Bleak House*, pp. 255–6. See also Harland S. Nelson, *Charles Dickens* (Boston, MA: Thayne Publishers, 1981) for a full discussion of Dickens's serial endings.

74 See Ofcom Broadcast Bulletin, 1 August 2011 for its report on viewers' complaints about this storyline. Available at stakeholders.ofcom.org.uk/binaries/ enforcement/broadcast-bulletins/obb187/ obb187.pdf.

75 See Dorothy Hobson, *Soap Opera* (Cambridge: Polity, 2003) for a detailed account of soap production.

76 Discussion between Stafford-Clark, Davies and White on DVD commentary for episode 11.

77 Pishiris, 'Do It Like Dickens', p. 22. Note that this pace of shooting is less frantic than on *EastEnders* where fifteen minutes of television a day are expected when shooting in the studio and eight a day on location (Hobson, *Soap Opera*, p. 30 onwards).

78 DVD commentary for episode 1, 11 and 15 gives production information of this kind.

79 Reprinted in Dyson, *Dickens Bleak House*, p. 57.

80 John, *Dickens and Mass Culture*, p. 189.

81 Grahame Smith, *Dickens, Money and Society* (Berkeley: University of California Press; Cambridge University Press, 1968), p. 136.

82 Smith, *Dickens, Money and Society*, p. 127.

83 DVD commentary, episode 11.

84 See my article 'Discussing Quality: Critical Vocabularies and Popular Television Drama', in James Curran and David Morley (eds), *Media and Cultural Theory* (Oxford: Routledge, 2006) for further discussion of the changes referred to here.

85 Cartmell and Whelehan, 'A Practical Understanding of Literature on Screen', p. 240; Giddings, 'Soft-soaping Dickens'; Cartmell and Whelehan, 'A Practical Understanding of Literature on Screen'; Conference of the Association of Adaptation Studies, Berlin, September 2010, personal notes.

86 Bryan Appleyard, '*Bleak House* the Soap? What the Dickens …', *Sunday Times*, 2 October 2005.

87 Sarah Cardwell, *Andrew Davies* (Manchester: Manchester University Press, 2005), p. 190.

88 David Lusted, 'Literary Adaptation and Cultural Fantasies', *Journal of Popular British Cinema* vol. 4, 2001, p. 75.

89 Julianne Pidduck, *Contemporary Costume Film: Space, Place and the Past* (London: BFI, 2004), p. 12.

90 Kamilla Elliott, *Rethinking the Novel/Film Debate* (Cambridge: Cambridge University Press, 2003), p.177.

91 Lisa Hopkins, 'The Red and the Blue; Jane Eyre in the 1990s', in Deborah Cartmell *et al*. (eds), *Classics in Film and Fiction* (London: Pluto, 2000), p. 69.

92 Reprinted in Dyson, *Dickens Bleak House*, p. 50.

93 Reprinted in Dyson, *Dickens Bleak House*, p. 57.

94 Reprinted in Dyson, *Dickens Bleak House*, p. 74.

95 Reprinted in Dyson, *Dickens Bleak House*, p. 87.

96 Reprinted in Dyson, *Dickens Bleak House*, p. 79.

97 Forster, *The Life of Charles Dickens*, p. 115.

98 A. E. Dyson, '*Bleak House*: Esther Better Not Born' reprinted in Dyson, *Dickens Bleak House*, pp. 262, 264, 265.

99 Vladimir Nabokov, '*Bleak House* 1852–3', in Michael Hollington (ed.), *Charles Dickens: Critical Assessments Volume III* (Mountfield: Helm Information, 1995), p. 175.

100 Robert Garis, *The Dickens Theatre: A Reassessment of the Novels* (Oxford: Clarendon Press, 1965), pp. 141–2.

101 John Carey, *The Violent Effigy* (London: Faber & Faber, 1973), p. 161; Angus Wilson cited in Jeremy Hawthorn (ed.), *Bleak House* (Basingstoke: Macmillan, 1987), p. 27.

102 Hawthorn, *Bleak House*, p. 38.

103 Q. D. Leavis, '*Bleak House*: A Chancery World', in F. R. Leavis and Q. D. Leavis, *Dickens: The Novelist* (London: Chatto & Windus, 1970), p. 83.

104 Leavis, *Bleak House*, pp. 154–9.

105 Grahame Smith, *Charles Dickens, Bleak House* (London: Edward Arnold, 1974), p. 16.

106 Carolyn Dever in *Death and the Mother* (1998), in Janice M. Allan (ed.), *Charles Dickens's Bleak House: A Sourcebook* (London and New York: Routledge, 2004), p. 90.

107 Virginia Blain, '*Bleak House*: A Feminist Perspective', in Harold Bloom (ed.), *Charles Dickens's Bleak House* (New York: Chelsea House Publishers, 1987), p. 142.

108 Alex Zederling, 'Esther Summerson Rehabilitated', *PMLA* vol. 88 no. 3, May 1973, pp. 429–30.

109 Anny Sadrin, 'Charlotte Dickens: The Female Narrator of *Bleak House*', in Hollington, *Charles Dickens*, p. 257.

110 Allan, *Charles Dickens's Bleak House*, p. 1.

111 Cartmell and Whelehan, 'A Practical Understanding of Literature on Screen', pp. 240–1.

112 Giddings, 'Soft-soaping Dickens'.

113 Cartmell and Whelehan, 'A Practical Understanding of Literature on Screen', p. 247.

123

114 Giddings, 'Soft-soaping Dickens'.
115 Giddings, 'Soft-soaping Dickens'.
116 Libby Duplock quoted in Aida
Edemariam, 'Dark Days in Albert Square',
Guardian, 13 September 2008.
117 Amy Taylor, 'NSPCC Reflect on
Eastenders' Coverage of Child Abuse',
Community Care, 23 September 2008.
118 Cartmell and Whelehan, 'A Practical
Understanding of Literature on Screen',
p. 242.
119 Cartmell and Whelehan, 'A Practical
Understanding of Literature on Screen',
p. 248.
120 Tzvetan Todorov, *The Poetics of Prose*
(New York: Cornell University Press, 1977),
p. 135.
121 Stone, *Dickens' Working Notes for His
Novels*, p. 231.
122 A. O. J. Cockshut, *The Imagination of
Charles Dickens* (London: Collins, 1961),
p. 133.
123 DVD commentary, episode 11.
124 J. Hillis Miller, 'The Interpretive Dance
in Charles Dickens's *Bleak House*' (1971)
in Bloom, *Charles Dickens's Bleak House*,
p. 22.
125 Stone, *Dickens' Working Notes for His
Novels*, p. 213.
126 Cartmell and Whelehan, 'A Practical
Understanding of Literature on Screen',
p. 245. After the opening episodes, scenes
did become longer, particularly as the story
needed to be embedded in, for instance,
episodes 4 and 5.
127 In the DVD commentary for episode 15
Davies indicates that he did not write this
ending and that it was developed by the
director, Susanna White.
128 Miriam Margoyles, 'Playing Dickens:
Miriam Margoyles. A Conversation with
John Galvin' in John Galvin (ed.), *Dickens
on Screen* (Cambridge: Cambridge
University Press, 2003), p. 105; and

Martin Jarvis in *Who Framed Charles
Dickens?*
129 See Christine Geraghty, 'The
Continuous Serial – A Definition', in R. Dyer
et al. (eds), *Coronation Street* (London:
BFI, 1981).
130 Smith, *Charles Dickens, Bleak House*,
p. 20.
131 J. Hillis Miller, *Charles Dickens:
The World of his Novels* (Bloomington:
Indiana University Press, 1969 (1958)),
pp. 180–1.
132 Hunter, *English Filming, English
Writing*, p. 173.
133 Dyson, *Dickens Bleak House*, p. 252;
Leavis, '*Bleak House*', p. 160; Allon H.
White, 'Language and Location in Charles
Dickens's *Bleak House*', in Hollington,
Charles Dickens, p. 223.
134 Caughie, *Television Drama*, p. 215.
135 Pishiris, 'Do It Like Dickens', p. 22.
136 Slater, *Charles Dickens*, p. 5; Ackroyd,
Dickens, p. 680.
137 Murray Baumgarten, 'Fictions of the
City', in John O. Jordan (ed.), *The
Cambridge Companion to Charles Dickens*
(Cambridge: Cambridge University Press,
2001), p. 106.
138 Slater, *Charles Dickens*, p. 322.
139 See Charlotte Brunsdon's *London in
Cinema* (London: BFI, 2007) for a full
discussion of landmark London and indeed
the London of the Thames.
140 This image suggests Miller's point
referenced above that many of the characters
live in self-enclosed 'ambience-bubbles'.
141 Jeremy Tambling, *Going Astray:
Dickens and London* (Harlow: Pearson
Longman, 2008), p. 140.
142 Miller, *Charles Dickens*, p. 204.
143 Slater, *Charles Dickens*, p. 344.
Jo and Esther have different diseases but
the metaphor works in a less than literal
way.

124

144 Andrew Davies, 'Andrew Davies on How to Adapt Literary Classics for TV', *Telegraph*, 18 February 2011.
145 Quoted in Jane R. Cohen, *Charles Dickens and His Illustrators* (Columbus: Ohio State University Press, 1980), p. 4.
146 Ackroyd, *Dickens*, pp. 589–90.
147 Grahame Smith, *Dickens and the Dream of Cinema* (Manchester: Manchester University Press, 2003), p. 164.
148 John Romano, 'Writing after Dickens: The Television Writer's Art' in Galvin, *Dickens on Screen*, p. 92.
149 Steig, *Dickens and Phiz*, p. 135; Cohen, *Charles Dickens and His Illustrators*, p. 9.
150 Steig, *Dickens and Phiz*, p. 157.
151 Steig, *Dickens and Phiz*, p. 157. Browne's illustrations are not universally admired and Richard L. Stein provides a concise summary of the commentary on them in 'Dickens and Illustration', in Jordan, *The Cambridge Companion to Charles Dickens* .
152 Hunter, *English Filming, English Writing*, p. 173.
153 Steig, *Dickens and Phiz*, p. 143.
154 Sarah Cardwell, 'Literature on the Small Screen: Television Adaptations', in Cartmell and Whelehan, *The Cambridge Companion to Literature on Screen*, p. 185.
155 Cardwell 'Literature on the Small Screen', p. 188.
156 Ian MacKillop and Alison Platt, ' "Beholding in a Magic Panorama": Television and the illustration of *Middlemarch*', in Robert Giddings and Erica Sheen (eds), *The Classic Novel: From Page to Screen* (Manchester: Manchester University Press, 2000), pp. 71–2.
157 John T. Caldwell, *Televisuality: Style, Crisis, and Authority in American Television* (New Brunswick, NJ: Rutgers University Press, 1995), p.4.
158 Smith, *Dickens and the Dream of Cinema*, p. 149.
159 Cardwell, 'Literature on the Small Screen', p. 184; Giddings, 'Soft-soaping Dickens'.
160 Hunter, *English Filming, English Writing*, p. 183.
161 Cardwell, 'Literature on the Small Screen', p. 190.
162 All quotations taken from 'Shooting in HD: It's All in the Detail', *Broadcast*, 28 July 2005.
163 Appleyard, '*Bleak House* the Soap?'.
164 Kleinecke-Bates (2006) demonstrates that there was an interest in new visual approaches to classic serials before *Bleak House*, quoting Chris Mentoul the director of ITV's *The Forsyte Saga* in 2002 on the use of long lenses to get close to the action and wide-angle lenses to give breadth.
165 *Independent*, 28 October 2005, p. 52.
166 Paul Hoggart, 'The Reality Is, Dickens Isn't Soap Opera', Features, *The Times*, 22 October 2005, p. 42.
167 Andrew Billen, 'Full of Vulgar Touches, This Adaptation Is Truly Dickensian', *New Statesman*, 31 October 2005; John Mullan, 'Will Bleak House Work as a Soap Opera?', *Scotsman*, 15 October 2005.
168 John Preston, *Sunday Telegraph*, Review, 30 October 2005, p. 10; Victor Lewis-Smith, *Evening Standard*, 25 November 2005. Both in BFI microfiche collection.
169 Ian Johns, 'Davies Cuts through the Dickensian Fog', *The Times*, 28 October 2005.
170 David Chater, 'TV Preview', *The Times*, 27 October 2005.
171 Kathryn Flett, 'Hot House', *Observer*, 30 October 2005; Gerard O'Donovan, 'The

Fog of Words Is Lifted to Reveal a Luminous Super-soap', *Daily Telegraph*, 28 October 2005; Johns, 'Davies Cuts through the Dickensian Fog'. It is worth bearing in mind the quality of these comments on Dickens's *Bleak House* when newspapers criticise the BBC for 'dumbing down'.

172 O'Donovan, 'The Fog of Words Is Lifted to Reveal a Luminous Super-soap'.

173 Johns, 'Davies Cuts through the Dickensian Fog'.

174 Simon Jenkins, 'A Tale of Two BBCs', *Guardian*, 11 November 2005.

175 Louttit, citing Davies in Appleyard, '*Bleak House* the Soap?', pp. 36–7.

176 Iris Kleinecke-Bates, 'Historicising the Classic Novel Adaptation: *Bleak House* (2005) and British Television Contexts', in Rachel Carroll (ed.), *Adaptation in Contemporary Culture: Textual Infidelities* (London: Continuum, 2009), pp. 115–16.

177 Caughie, 'Television and Serial Fictions', pp. 21–2, 63–5.

178 Rebecca Arwen White, 'The Classic-Novel Adaptation from 1995 to 2009' (Durham University, 2010), p. 209.

179 White, 'The Classic-Novel Adaptation from 1995 to 2009', pp. 238–41. White

devotes an illuminating and detailed chapter to Dickens's adaptations from 1998 to 2008.

180 Quoted in Appleyard, '*Bleak House* the Soap?'.

181 Hensher, 'You'll Never Catch Me Watching It'.

182 Johns, 'Davies Cuts through the Dickensian Fog'.

183 Billen, 'Full of Vulgar Touches'.

184 Caughie, 'Televison and Serial Fictions', p. 63.

185 Kleinecke-Bates, 'Historicising the Classic Novel Adaptation', p. 116.

186 Eileen Lewis, *Teaching Television at GCSE* (London: Palgrave Macmillan, 2008), pp. 90–5.

187 The list was created by asking members of the television industry to vote on a list of possible programmes. It can be found at www.bfi.org.uk/features/tv/100/articles/drama_series.

188 See a number of articles in *Critical Studies in Television* vol. 4 no. 2, 2009 which debate the term 'classic' and its application to television.

189 Mark Thompson, 25 April 2006, at annual conference of the Voice of the Listener and Viewer.

190 Giddings, 'Soft-soaping Dickens'.

Appendix 1: The Beginning and Ending of Each Episode

Episode 1: the inn from which Esther is picked up; Tulkinghorn's face after finding Nemo dead.

Episode 2: Tulkinghorn outside Nemo's room; long shot of Lady Dedlock in her bedroom.

Episode 3: the house which Guppy is standing outside, looking for Esther; Esther smiles while holding Allan's posy.

Episode 4: corridor at Kenge and Carboy's as Richard arrives; Tulkinghorn's face after Jo says 'That's the lady.'

Episode 5: Jo's face; Richard's face after Gridley's death.

Episode 6: corridor in Tulkinghorn's house as George arrives; Esther's face after she hears of Jo's disappearance.

Episode 7: long shot of Bleak House as the search for Jo begins; George's face as he leaves Tulkinghorn's office.

Episode 8: long shot of George's shooting gallery; Esther's face as she weeps in her bedroom.

Episode 9: long shot of Lady Dedlock looking out; Tulkinghorn's face watching Lady Dedlock go down the corridor.

Episode 10: long shot of carriage in countryside; George's face after he threatens Tulkinghorn.

Episode 11: long shot of Bleak House; Tulkinghorn's dead face.

Episode 12: Clamb (Tom Georgeson) in Tulkinghorn's house; the note reading 'Lady Dedlock – murderess'.

Episode 13: close-up of handle of bell; Hortense's face at her arrest.

Episode 14: close-up of hand of Hortense; Esther embraces Lady Dedlock at gate of graveyard.

Episode 15: long shot of horses pulling a carriage; close-up of Esther and Allan kissing.

Many of these shots are very short and involve camera movement or zoom.

Bibliography

Ackroyd, Peter, *Dickens* (London: Random House, 1991).

Allan, Janice M. (ed.), *Charles Dickens's Bleak House: A Sourcebook* (London and New York: Routledge, 2004).

Appleyard, Bryan, '*Bleak House* the Soap? What the Dickens ...', *Sunday Times*, 2 October 2005.

Armstrong, Stephen, 'Under the Wire', *Media Guardian*, 6 April 2009.

Baumgarten, Murray, 'Fictions of the City', in John O. Jordan (ed.), *The Cambridge Companion to Charles Dickens* (Cambridge: Cambridge University Press, 2001).

Billen, Andrew, 'Full of Vulgar Touches, This Adaptation Is Truly Dickensian', *New Statesman*, 31 October 2005, www.newstatesman.com/200510310044.

Blain, Virginia, '*Bleak House*: A Feminist Perspective', in Harold Bloom (ed.), *Charles Dickens's Bleak House* (New York: Chelsea House Publishers, 1987).

Brunsdon, Charlotte, *London in Cinema* (London: BFI, 2007).

Butt, John and Tillotson, Elizabeth, *Dickens at Work* (London: Methuen, 1957).

Byrne, Ciar, 'What the Dickens! BBC Rebuilds "Bleak House" for the Hollyoaks Generation', *Independent*, 5 October 2005.

Caldwell, John T., *Televisuality: Style, Crisis, and Authority in American Television* (New Brunswick, NJ: Rutgers University Press, 1995).

Cardwell, Sarah, *Adaptation Revisited: Television and the Classic Novel* (Manchester: Manchester University Press, 2002).

Cardwell, Sarah, *Andrew Davies* (Manchester: Manchester University Press, 2005).

Cardwell, Sarah, 'Literature on the Small Screen: Television Adaptations', in Deborah Cartmell and Imelda Whelehan (eds), *The Cambridge Companion to Literature on Screen* (Cambridge: Cambridge University Press, 2007).

Carey, John, *The Violent Effigy* (London: Faber & Faber, 1973).

Cartmell, Deborah and Whelehan, Imelda, 'A Practical Understanding of Literature on Screen: Two Conversations with Andrew Davies', in Deborah Cartmell and Imelda Whelehan (eds), *The Cambridge Companion to Literature on Screen* (Cambridge: Cambridge University Press, 2007).

Caughie, John, *Television Drama: Realism, Modernism, and British Culture* (Oxford: Oxford University Press, 2000).

Caughie, John, 'Television and Serial Fictions', in David Glover and Scott McCracken (eds), *The Cambridge Companion to Popular Fiction* (Cambridge: Cambridge University Press, 2012 forthcoming).

Chater, David, 'TV Preview', *The Times*, 27 October 2005.

Cockshut, A. O. J, *The Imagination of Charles Dickens* (London: Collins, 1961).

Cohen, Jane R., *Charles Dickens and His Illustrators* (Columbus: Ohio State University Press, 1980).

Collins, Philip (ed.), *Dickens: The Critical Heritage* (London: Routledge & Kegan Paul, 1971).

Critical Studies in Television vol. 4 no. 2, 2009.

Davies, Andrew, 'Critical Dedlock', *Guardian Unlimited*, 9 November 2005, www.guardian.co.uk/culture/culture vultureblog/2005/nov/09/criticaldedloc.

Davies, Andrew, 'Andrew Davies on How to Adapt Literary Classics for TV', *Telegraph*, 18 February 2011, www.telegraph.co.uk/culture/tvandradio/ 8328055/Andrew-Davies-on-how-to-adapt-literary-classics-for-TV.html.

Dickens, Charles, 'Preface', *Bleak House* (New York: Norton & Co., 1977).

Dyson, A. E. (ed.), *Dickens Bleak House: A Casebook* (London: Macmillan, 1969).

Dyson, A. E., '*Bleak House*: Esther Better Not Born?' (1969) reprinted in Dyson, *Dickens Bleak House*.

Edemariam, Aida, 'Dark Days in Albert Square', *Guardian*, 13 September 2008, www.guardian.co.uk/media/ 2008/ sep/13/eastenders.television.

Elliott, Kamilla, *Rethinking the Novel/Film Debate* (Cambridge: Cambridge University Press, 2003).

Feuer, Jane, 'HBO and the Concept of Quality TV', in Janet McCabe and Kim Akass (eds), *Quality TV: Contemporary American Television and Beyond* (London and New York : I. B. Tauris, 2007).

Flett, Kathryn, 'Hot House', *Observer*, 30 October 2005.

Forster, John, *The Life of Charles Dickens* (London: Dent, 1969).

Garis, Robert, *The Dickens Theatre: A Reassessment of the Novels* (Oxford: Clarendon Press, 1965).

Geraghty, Christine, 'The Continuous Serial – A Definition', in R. Dyer, C. Geraghty, T. Lovell, M. Jordan, R. Paterson and J. Stewart (eds), *Coronation Street* (London: BFI, 1981).

Geraghty, Christine, 'Discussing Quality: Critical Vocabularies and Popular Television Drama', in James Curran and David Morley (eds), *Media and Cultural Theory* (Oxford: Routledge, 2006).

Geraghty, Christine, *Now a Major Motion Picture: Film Adaptations from Literature and Drama* (Lanham, MD: Rowman & Littlefield, 2008).

Giddings, Robert, 'Soft-soaping Dickens: Andrew Davies, BBC 1 and Bleak House', on David Purdue's Charles Dickens Page (2004), charlesdickenspage.com/ Soft_Soaping_Dickens.html.

Giddings, Robert and Selby, Keith, *The Classic Serial on Television and Radio* (Basingstoke: Palgrave, 2001).

Harvey, W. J., '*Bleak House*: The Double Narrative', in Dyson, *Dickens Bleak House*.

Hawthorn, Jeremy (ed.), *Bleak House* (Basingstoke: Macmillan, 1987).

Hensher, Philip, 'You'll Never Catch Me Watching It', *Guardian*, 7 November 2005. www.guardian.co.uk/media/ 2005/nov/07/broadcasting.arts.

Hobson, Dorothy, *Soap Opera* (Cambridge: Polity, 2003).

Hoggart, Paul, 'The Reality Is, Dickens Isn't Soap Opera', *The Times*, Features, 22 October 2005.

Hopkins, Lisa, 'The Red and the Blue: Jane Eyre in the 1990s', in Deborah Cartmell *et al.* (eds), *Classics in Film and Fiction* (London: Pluto, 2000).

Hunter, Jefferson, *English Filming, English Writing* (Bloomington: Indiana University Press, 2010).

Jenkins, Simon, 'A Tale of Two BBCs', *Guardian*, 11 November 2005.

129

John, Juliet, *Dickens and Mass Culture* (Oxford: Oxford University Press, 2010).

Johns, Ian, 'Davies Cuts through the Dickensian Fog', *The Times*, 28 October 2005.

Kleinecke-Bates, Iris, 'Victorian Realities: Representations of the Victorian Age on 1990s British Television' (University of Warwick, 2006).

Kleinecke-Bates, Iris, 'Historicising the Classic Novel Adaptation: *Bleak House* (2005) and British Television Contexts', in Rachel Carroll (ed.), *Adaptation in Contemporary Culture: Textual Infidelities* (London: Continuum, 2009).

Leavis, Q. D., '*Bleak House*: A Chancery World', in F. R. Leavis and Q. D. Leavis, *Dickens: The Novelist* (London: Chatto & Windus, 1970).

Levine, Caroline, 'From Genre to Form: A Response to Jason Mittell on *The Wire*', www.electonicbookreview.com/ thread/firstperson/serial.

Lewis, Eileen, *Teaching Television at GCSE* (London: Palgrave Macmillan, 2008).

Lewis-Smith, Victor, *Evening Standard*, 25 November 2005.

Louttit, Chris, '*Cranford*, Popular Culture and the Politics of Adapting the Victorian Novel', *Adaptation* vol. 2 no. 1, 2009.

Lusted, David, 'Literary Adaptation and Cultural Fantasies', *Journal of Popular British Cinema* vol. 4, 2001.

MacKillop, Ian and Platt, Alison, ' "Beholding in a Magic Panorama": Television and the Illustration of *Middlemarch*', in Robert Giddings and Erica Sheen (eds), *The Classic Novel: From Page to Screen* (Manchester: Manchester University Press, 2000).

Margoyles, Miriam, 'Playing Dickens: Miriam Margoyles: A Conversation with John Galvin', in John Galvin (ed.), *Dickens on Screen* (Cambridge: Cambridge University Press, 2003).

Miller, David A., 'Discipline in Different Voices: Bureaucracy, Police, Family and *Bleak House*', in Michael Hollington (ed.), *Charles Dickens: Critical Assessments, Volume III* (Mountfield: Helm Information, 1995).

Miller, J. Hillis, *Charles Dickens: The World of His Novels* (Bloomington: Indiana University Press, 1969 (1958)).

Miller, J. Hillis, 'The Interpretive Dance in Charles Dickens's *Bleak House*' (1971), in Harold Bloom (ed.), *Charles Dickens's Bleak House* (New York: Chelsea House Publishers, 1987).

Mullan, John, 'Will Bleak House Work as a Soap Opera?', *Scotsman*, 15 October 2005.

Nabokov, Vladimir, '*Bleak House* 1852–3', in Michael Hollington (ed.), *Charles Dickens: Critical Assessments, Volume III* (Mountfield: Helm Information, 1995).

Nelson, Harland S., *Charles Dickens* (Boston, MA: Thayne Publishers, 1981).

Nelson, Robin, *State of Play: Contemporary 'High-End' TV Drama* (Manchester: Manchester University Press, 2007).

O'Donovan, Gerard, 'The Fog of Words Is Lifted to Reveal a Luminous Super-soap', *Telegraph*, 28 October 2005.

Pidduck, Julianne, *Contemporary Costume Film: Space, Place and the Past* (London: BFI, 2004).

Pishiris, Christina, 'Do It Like Dickens', *Televisual*, August 2005.

Pointer, Michael, *Charles Dickens on the Screen* (London and Lanham, MD: Scarecrow Press, 1996).

Preston, John, *Sunday Telegraph*, Review, 30 October 2005.

Richards, Jeffrey, *Films and British National Identity: From Dickens to Dad's*

Army (Manchester: Manchester University Press, 1997).

Romano, John, 'Writing after Dickens: The Television Writer's Art', in John Galvin (ed.), *Dickens on Screen* (Cambridge: Cambridge University Press, 2003).

Sadrin, Anny, 'Charlotte Dickens: The Female Narrator of *Bleak House*', in Michael Hollington (ed.), *Charles Dickens: Critical Assessments, Volume III* (Mountfield: Helm Information, 1995).

Slater, Michael, *Charles Dickens* (New Haven, CT and London: Yale University Press, 2011).

Smith, Grahame, *Dickens, Money and Society* (Berkeley: University of California Press; Cambridge University Press, 1968).

Smith, Grahame, *Charles Dickens, Bleak House* (London: Edward Arnold, 1974).

Smith, Grahame, *Charles Dickens: A Literary Life* (Basingstoke: Macmillan, 1996).

Smith, Grahame, *Dickens and the Dream of Cinema* (Manchester: Manchester University Press, 2003).

Steig, Michael, *Dickens and Phiz* (Bloomington and London: Indiana University Press, 1978).

Stein, Richard L., 'Dickens and Illustration', in John O. Jordan (ed.), *The Cambridge Companion to Charles Dickens* (Cambridge: Cambridge University Press, 2001).

Stone, Harry (ed), *Dickens' Working Notes for His Novels* (Chicago, IL: University of Chicago Press, 1987).

Storey, Graham, *Charles Dickens, Bleak House* (Cambridge: Cambridge University Press, 1987).

Tambling, Jeremy, *Going Astray: Dickens and London* (Harlow: Pearson Longman, 2008).

Taylor, Amy, 'NSPCC Reflect on *EastEnders*' Coverage of Child Abuse', *Community Care*, 23 December 2008. www.communitycare.co.uk/Articles/23/12/2008/110283/NSPCC-reflect-on-Eastenders39-coverage-of-child-abuse.htm.

Todorov, Tzvetan, *The Poetics of Prose* (New York: Cornell University Press, 1977).

White, Allon H., 'Language and Location in Charles Dickens's *Bleak House*', in Michael Hollington (ed.), *Charles Dickens: Critical Assessments, Volume III* (Mountfield: Helm Information, 1995).

White, Rebecca Arwen, 'The Classic-Novel Adaptation from 1995 to 2009', (Durham University, 2010), Durham E-Theses Online, etheses.dur.ac.uk/443/.

Zederling, Alex, 'Esther Summerson Rehabilitated', *PMLA* vol. 88 no. 3, May 1973.

Credits

Bleak House

**United Kingdom/USA
2005**

directed by
Justin Chadwick [1–9]
Susanna White [10–15]
produced by
Nigel Stafford-Clark
screenplay by
Andrew Davies
[based on the novel]
Bleak House
by Charles Dickens
director of photography
Kieran McGuigan
editors
Paul Knight [1–9]
Jason Krasucki [10–15]
production designer
Simon Elliott
composer
John Lunn

©2005. BBC
production companies
a BBC, WGBH Boston
co-production in association
with Deep Indigo
executive producers
Sally Haynes
Laura Mackie
executive producer for WGBH
Rebecca Eaton
line producer
Alison Barnett
production executive
Gordon Ronald
production co-ordinator
Dani Gordon
assistant co-ordinator
Clare Jones
location managers
Nick Wade
Nick Marshall
unit manager
Sharon McGuinness

production secretary
Sarah Irvine
production runner
Nick Tanner
production accountant
Simon Windsor
assistant accountants
Georgina Kelly
Polly Fletcher
first assistant directors
Steve Robinson [1–9]
Nige Watson [10–15]
second assistant director
Alison Banks
third assistant director
Emma Stokes
additional assistant director
Marcia Gay
crowd co-ordinator
Harriet Worth
floor runner
Carley Lane
script supervisor
Jayne Spooner
casting
Kate Rhodes James
casting assistant
Andy Morgan
script editors
Ellie Wood [1–10]
Caroline Skinner [1–15]
A camera operator [1]/camera
[2–15]
Ian Adrian
B camera operator
Paul Donachie
additional camera operators
Luke Redgrave
Peter Field
focus
Russell Ferguson
Rory Moles
camera assistant
Nicky George
additional camera assistant
Andreas Pepe
gaffer
Mark Clayton

best boy
Benny Harper
electricians
Dave Campbell
Enrico Faccio
Chris Tann
generator operator
Tony Tyler
grip
Barry Read
stills
Mike Hogan
special effects supervisor
Neal Champion
visual effects
Oliver Money
Ric Comline
post-production supervisor
Beewan Athwal
on-line editor
Shane Warden
assembly editor
Jim Hampton
art director
Bill Crutcher
standby art director
Suzanne Austin
art department assistant
Charlie Lynam
production buyer
Annie Gilhooly
assistant buyer
Sarah Duncan
graphic designer
Martin Lang
property master
Peter Hallam
props
Malcolm Bensted
Harry Cable
Colin Bayliss
Oli van der Vijver
Steve Thompson
rigger
Mickey Coveney
standby rigger
Reg Martin

standby painter
Jesse Hammond
standby carpenters
Peter Cooper
Alan Sprawson
construction manager
Dan Crandon
scenic artist
Gillian Campbell
construction
Tim Crowdy
Bruce Barnes
Jason Htay
Tim Powis
costume designer
Andrea Galer
assistant costume designer
Charlotte Morris
costume supervisor
Sally Crees
crowd costume
Sarah Touaibi
costume
Claire Collins
Mark Lord
make-up and hair designer
Daniel Phillips
make-up/hair supervisor
Tapio Salmi
make-up/hair
Rebecca Cole
Kay Bilk
Joe Hopker
crowd make-up/hair co-ordinator
Beverley Binda
title design
Peter Anderson
colourist
Chris Beeton
choreographer
Paul Harris
sound recordists
Chris Ashworth [1–15]
Sandy Macrae [10–15]
sound maintenance
Mike Reardon
Adrienne Taylor
supervising sound editor
Stephen Griffiths
dialogue editor
Ian Wilkinson
dubbing mixer
Stuart Hilliker

stunt co-ordinators
Andy Bradford
Nrinder Dhudwar
fencing masters
William Hobbs
Richard Bonehill
consultant
Jenny Uglow

Main Cast
Gillian Anderson
Lady Honoria Dedlock
Alun Armstrong
Bucket
Lilo Baur
Hortense
Charlie Brooks
Jenny
Warren Clarke
Lawrence Boythorn
Pauline Collins
Miss Flite
Dermot Crowley
Mr Vholes
Charles Dance
Mr Tulkinghorn
Tim Dantay
Mr Rouncewell
Joanna David
Mrs Badger
Phil Davis
Smallweed
Bryan Dick
Prince Turveydrop
Harry Eden
Jo
Tom Georgeson
Clamb
Burn Gorman
William Guppy
Richard Griffiths
Mr Bayham Badger
Sheila Hancock
Mrs Guppy
Richard Harrington
Allan Woodcourt
Tony Haygarth
Gridley
Matthew Kelly
old Turveydrop
Patrick Kennedy
Richard Carstone
Denis Lawson
John Jarndyce

John Lynch
Nemo
Anna Maxwell Martin
Esther Summerson
Sean McGinley
Snagsby
Alistair McGowan
Mr Kenge
Carey Mulligan
Ada Clare
Nathaniel Parker
Harold Skimpole
Natalie Press
Caddy Jellaby
Robert Pugh
Mr Chadband
Anne Reid
Mrs Rouncewell
Ian Richardson
Chancellor
Michael Smiley
Phil Squod
Hugo Speer
Sergeant George
Liza Tarbuck
Mrs Jellaby
Catherine Tate
Mrs Chadband
Roberta Taylor
Mrs Pardiggle
Johnny Vegas
Krook
Timothy West
Sir Leicester Dedlock

and – in order of appearance
episode 1
Anthony Cozens
usher
Sevan Stephan
Mr Tangle
Alastair Galbraith
Mr Brownlow
Ruby Williams
little Esther
Kelly Hunter
Miss Barbary
John Sheahan
Fortnum
Lisa Hammond
Harriet
Emma Williams
Rosa

133

Rod Arthur
Neckett
Andy Linden
pawnbroker
Cosh Omar
brickmaker
Tim Bruce
angry man

episode 2
Peter Guinness
coroner
Paul Sirr
clergyman
Emma Williams
Rosa

episode 3
Emily Jewell
servant London lodgings
Alastair Galbraith
Mr Brownlow
Anthony Cozens
usher
Sevan Stephan
Mr Tangle
Amelda Brown
landlady
Billy Hill
Tom Neckett
Katie Angelou
Charley Neckett
Lisa Hammond
Harriet

episode 4
Sally Leonard
Polly
Keith Bartlett
vicar
Emma Williams
Rosa
Michelle Tate
Guster
Dominic Coleman
policeman in Snagsby's
Mary Sheen
old woman

episode 5
Katie Angelou
Charley Neckett
Loo Brealey
Judy

Sevan Stephan
Mr Tangle
Alastair Galbraith
Mr Brownlow

episode 6
Emma Williams
Rosa
Lisa Hammond
Harriet
Di Botcher
Mrs Woodcourt
Levi Hayes
young Smallweed
Katie Angelou
Charley Neckett
Richard Cant
Mercury

episode 7
Katie Angelou
Charley Neckett
Lisa Hammond
Harriet
Benedict Martin
policeman outside Krook's
Peter Guinness
coroner
Richard Cant
Mercury

episode 8
Katie Angelou
Charley Neckett
Loo Brealey
Judy
Alex Blake
countryman
Lila Sharp
little girl

episode 9
Emma Williams
Rosa
Patrick Monckton
Mr Grubble
Loo Brealey
Judy
Katie Angelou
Charley Neckett
Anthony Cozens
usher
Alastair Galbraith
Mr Brownlow

Sevan Stephan
Mr Tangle

episode 10
Emma Williams
Rosa
Lisa Hammond
Harriet
Loo Brealey
Judy

episode 11
Emma Williams
Rosa
Barry Ewart
Deal innkeeper
Benedict Martin
policeman outside Snagsby's
Katie Angelou
Charley Neckett
Richard Cant
Mercury

episode 12
Loo Brealey
Judy
Richard Cant
Mercury
Howard Coggins
policeman at Tulkinghorn's
Brian Pettyfer
Mr Growler
Emily Jewell
servant London lodgings

episode 13
Richard Cant
Mercury
Lisa Hammond
Harriet
Loo Brealey
Judy
Richard Pettyfer
constable at Dedlock's

episode 14
Richard Pettyfer
constable at Dedlock's
Jack Brough
constable at station
Loo Brealey
Judy
Richard Cant
Mercury

134

John Sheahan
Fortnum
Katie Angelou
Charley Neckett

episode 15
Loo Brealey
Judy
Katie Angelou
Charley Neckett
Tony Guilfoyle
lawyer
Anthony Cozens
usher
Di Botcher
Mrs Woodcourt

production details
filmed from 7 February to
15 July 2005 (21 shooting
weeks) on location in
Hertfordshire, Bedfordshire,
Kent, Lincolnshire, Essex and
London (England) and at BBC
Elstree Studios (Hertfordshire,
England). filmed on HDCAM
(1.78:1). Budget reported as
£6,000,000

transmission history
episode 1 BBC1
27 October 2005
(20.00–21.00)
57m 11s
episode 2 BBC1
28 October 2005
(20.30–21.00)
29m 19s
episode 3 BBC1
3 November 2005
(20.00–20.30)
29m 4s
episode 4 BBC1
4 November 2005
(20.30–21.00)
29m 18s
episode 5 BBC1
10 November 2005
(20.00–20.30)
29m 18s
episode 6 BBC1
11 November 2005
(20.30–21.00)
29m 18s
episode 7 BBC1
17 November 2005
(20.00–20.30)
29m 18s
episode 8 BBC1
24 November 2005
(20.00–20.30)
29m 18s

episode 9 BBC1
25 November 2005
(20.30–21.00)
29m 9s
episode 10 BBC1
1 December 2005
(20.00–20.30)
29m 16s
episode 11 BBC1
2 December 2005
(20.30–21.00)
29m 17s
episode 12 BBC1
8 December 2005
(20.00–20.30)
29m 11s
episode 13 BBC1
9 December 2005
(20.30–21.00)
29m 18s
episode 14 BBC1
15 December 2005
(20.00–20.30)
29m 17s
episode 15 BBC1
16 December 2005
(20.30–21.00)
29m 12s

135

Index

Note: Page numbers in **bold** indicate detailed analysis; those in *italic* refer to illustrations; *n* = endnote.

138

139

Also Published:

Buffy the Vampire Slayer
Anne Billson

Civilisation
Jonathan Conlin

Cracker
Mark Duguid

CSI: Crime Scene Investigation
Steven Cohan

Deadwood
Jason Jacobs

Doctor Who
Kim Newman

Edge of Darkness
John Caughie

Law and Order
Charlotte Brunsdon

The League of Gentlemen
Leon Hunt

The Likely Lads
Phil Wickham

The Office
Ben Walters

Our Friends in the North
Michael Eaton

Prime Suspect
Deborah Jermyn

Queer as Folk
Glyn Davis

Seinfeld
Nicholas Mirzoeff

Seven Up
Stella Bruzzi

The Singing Detective
Glen Creeber

Star Trek
Ina Rae Hark